MINISTRY TO THE SICK AND DYING

By

Dr. Mary Ann Braham

© 2002 by Dr. Mary Ann Braham. All rights reserved.

No part of this book may be reproduced, stored in a retrieval system, or transmitted by any means, electronic, mechanical, photocopying, recording, or otherwise, without written permission from the author.

ISBN: 1-4033-5896-6 (e-book)
ISBN: 1-4033-5897-4 (Paperback)
ISBN: 1-4033-5898-2 (Hardcover)

Library of Congress Control Number: 2002093557

This book is printed on acid free paper.

Printed in the United States of America
Bloomington, IN

1stBooks - rev. 10/04/02

Dedication

This book is dedicated to all of my family and friends who have supported me in my ministry. A special thanks to my husband, Larry, for always encouraging me to, "Go for it!" I would also like to thank my sons, Jeremy and Nick and grandson Cody, for their inspiration in this endeavor. A special thanks also goes to Cathy who is always there with an encouraging word when I'm ready to give up.

I'd also like to thank Dr. Harley Howard of the Foundations of Truth Bible Church for all his help and guidance along the way.

A special thanks goes to my CPE group and our supervisor, Karen Morrow. Karen taught me most of what I know about chaplaincy.

Ministry to the Sick and Dying

TABLE OF CONTENTS

Ministry to the Sick and Dying

Introduction

This book is intended to be an introduction to the ministry to those who are sick or dying. I strongly encourage all those entering the ministry to take a unit of Clinical Pastoral Education (CPE) for experience.

An important part of a pastor's role in the church is to shepherd the flock. This includes ministering to the sick and dying. Some large churches have a staff pastor whose sole call is to minister to flock. Most churches, however, do not have a pastor whose sole responsibility is pastoral care, so that responsibility falls on the senior pastor. It is important to know how to minister to those who are at this point where they may have a tremendous spiritual need. It is easy for a pastor who has had no training in this area to say or do something that will cause harm to the patient either emotionally or spiritually.

Jesus had a special place in His heart for those who were sick, disfigured by disease, or threatened with death. God's compassion for all His children is revealed in the human touch of Jesus Christ. Jesus touched many both physically and spiritually, breaking through the diseases that made them outcasts from society. If these people were important to Jesus, shouldn't they be important to us as well? Shouldn't we make a special effort to minister to those who are sick or dying? Should we not bring God's love into their hearts?

This book is intended to be a guideline for those in this ministry, whether lay or pastoral. I will give simple, easy to understand guides as well as examples. It is my hope that all those who read this book will be better equipped to provide spiritual care for those who are sick or dying.

The material used in writing this book comes mainly from my experience. I have also incorporated what I have learned from CPE, which I took at a government research facility. I will cite some articles throughout the course and some works that would help in your study.

Throughout my life, God has been preparing me for ministry to the sick and dying. It began when I was only five and my paternal grandma and maternal great-grandma went home to the Lord. I watched my dad die from cancer when I was in my teens, followed by my granddad, who died from a heart attack. My son battled cancer when he was in his teens. The point at which I heard the call was when I cared for my maternal grandma during her bout with cancer and her passing away. I have received comfort from the Lord throughout these losses in my life. It is my prayer that I can pass along what I have learned so that others may minister and share God's comfort with others.

I have accepted 2 Corinthians 1:3-4 as my life's mission. I believe that God has prepared me to minister to the sick through the trials throughout my lifetime. I want to share the comfort that I have received with those who are going through similar trials, and illness. I believe this is part of God's plan for us.

2 Cor. 1:3-4

Blessed *be* God, even the Father of our Lord Jesus Christ, the
Father of mercies, and the God of all comfort; 4Who comforteth us in
all our tribulation, that we may be able to comfort them which are in
any trouble, by the comfort wherewith we ourselves are comforted of
God.

CHAPTER ONE

THE SHEPHERD

A special thanks to my brother, Dr. Harley Howard, for his work on the pastor as shepherd. Dr. Harley is a professor at Andersonville Baptist Seminary and pastor of Foundation of Truth Bible Church in California.

The pastor is the shepherd of the flock. Shepherd literally means the one who cares for the flock. Scripture tells us a lot about how the pastor is to care for the flock. Scripture parallels the way a shepherd cares for his flock to the way a pastor is to care for God's flock that is under his care. Following is a description of an earthly shepherd. "In the morning the shepherd would lead his fold from the flock, which he did by going before them and calling them by name. Arriving at the pasture, he watched the flock with the assistance of sheep dogs, and should any sheep stray, he searched for it until he found it. He led them to water, either to a running stream or troughs attached to wells. In the evening he made sure that none was missing as they passed under the rod as they entered the door of the sheepfold. He acted as the doorkeeper of the sheepfold, watching the fold at night, sometimes sleeping at the entrance of the sheepfold.

The shepherd's office required great watchfulness, especially at night, great tenderness toward the young and feeble sheep, especially when driving them to and from the pasture.

The shepherd's life involved much hardship and danger. Oftentimes shepherds lived in complete seclusion for the care of the sheep. The shepherd was exposed to the extremes of the weather and he did not eat much. He encountered attacks of wild beasts, robbers, and predators.

With all the dangers surrounding the shepherd and the sheep, his only weapons were a slingshot and a staff. His robe was made of sheepskin, and he had a pouch containing a small amount of food."

Being the shepherd of God's flock is not an easy task either. Jesus gives us a beautiful example of His great care for His sheep and leaves some precious illustrations of how pastors, as shepherds of Gods flock, can properly care for them.

John 10:1-5

Verily, verily, I say unto you, He that entereth not by the door into
the sheepfold, but climbeth up some other way, the same is a thief and
a robber. 2But he that entereth in by the door is the shepherd of the
sheep. 3To him the porter openeth; and the sheep hear his voice: and
he calleth his own sheep by name, and leadeth them out. 4And when
he putteth forth his own sheep, he goeth before them, and the sheep
follow him: for they know his voice. 5And a stranger will they not
follow, but will flee from him: for they know not the voice of
strangers.

Verses 1-2: The sheepfold was a roofless stall that was near the shepherd's home. It was walled by stone and had only one door. Any attempt to enter into the sheepfold by any other way other than the door was clearly an attempt by robbers. Those who are not God's true shepherds are those who will destroy churches. This is their prime objective. Genuine sheep of God will not follow the voice of one other than a true shepherd of God.

Verses 3-4: These verses give us much insight into the nature of both shepherd and sheep.

1. **Genuine sheep listen for the shepherd's voice.** Not everyone who claims to bc a sheep is a sheep. There are characteristics that reveal the nature of a true sheep of the Lord. True sheep listen for the shepherd's voice. **The sheep hear his voice.** They comprehend the voice of the shepherd.

2. **True shepherding involves responsibility for the sheep. He calleth HIS OWN sheep by name.** This should also imply that our first calling, as Pastors, is to the sheep, not to other ventures all over the place, leaving the sheep susceptible to all kinds of robbers, predators and animals ready to destroy the sheepfold. **HE CALLETH HIS OWN SHEEP BY NAME.** The sheep are the pastor's responsibility. Pastors have been entrusted with their care.

Acts 20:28

Take heed therefore unto yourselves, and to all the flock, over the which the Holy Ghost hath made you overseers, to feed the church of God, which he hath purchased with his own blood.

3. **True Shepherding involves <u>involvement</u> with the sheep. HE CALLETH HIS OWN SHEEP <u>BY NAME</u>.** The shepherd knew his own sheep **<u>PERSONALLY</u>**. You **cannot** be a shepherd in name only; you **<u>must</u>** involve your life with the sheep and must become **personally** involved with them. Let me say again and again and again, only God's sheep follow shepherds, goats do not. When we recognize who the sheep truly are, and we will if we become personally involved, then it is imperative that we become **personally** involved with the sheep.

4. **True shepherding involves <u>leadership</u>. AND HE <u>LEADETH</u> THEM OUT.** God's sheep follow shepherds; goats do not **(Read verse 4).**

John 10:4

And when he putteth forth his own sheep, he goeth before them, and the sheep follow him: for they know his voice.

5. **Genuine sheep are <u>involved</u> with the shepherd. THE SHEEP FOLLOW HIM.** Just as much as the shepherd needs to be involved with the lives of the sheep, the sheep also need to be involved in the life of the shepherd.

6. **Genuine sheep will <u>not</u> follow the voice of someone <u>other</u> than the shepherd. (Read verse 5).**

John 10:5

And a stranger will they not follow, but will flee from him: for they know not the voice of strangers.

God's sheep follow the shepherd's voice, goats do not. True sheep may be described a dumb animals by many, but they do have one characteristic that makes them very wise. They know who to follow and who not to follow. God's sheep have discernment to follow only the voice of true shepherds. They will not follow anyone who does not **speak for God**. They will not allow themselves to be **deceived** by false voices.

Jeremiah 23:1-4

1 Woe be unto the pastors that **destroy** and **scatter** the sheep of my pasture! saith the LORD.

The Lord sent a warning of **woe**, to those pastors who **caused my people to perish, who killed my sheep, who caused my sheep to go astray, to abandoned the sheep.**

2 Therefore thus saith the LORD God of Israel against the pastors that feed my people; Ye have scattered my flock, and driven them away, and have not visited them: behold, I will visit upon you the evil of your doings, saith the LORD.

God said that you have **pushed aside** my sheep and have **not** paid any attention to **their** needs. God said that He will **pay them back** for the wickedness of their deeds.

3 And I will gather the remnant of my flock out of all countries whither I have driven them, and will bring them again to their folds; and they shall be fruitful and increase.

4 And I will set up shepherds over them, which shall feed them: and they shall fear no more, nor be dismayed, neither shall they be lacking, saith the LORD.

God said, **I** will raise up **shepherds which shall shepherd you** and the sheep will have no need to be **broken**, nor will they be any **missing** sheep.

7. **Genuine sheep <u>know</u> the danger of following the voice of someone not familiar with them, the shepherd, and will <u>run</u> from them. (read verse 5).**

John 10:5

And a stranger will they not follow, but will flee from him: for they know not the voice of strangers.

The word, flee means to run like a fugitive from danger.

Acts 20:28-31

Acts 20:28-31

Take heed therefore unto yourselves, and to all the flock, over the
which the Holy Ghost hath made you overseers, to feed the church of
God, which he hath purchased with his own blood. 29For I know this,
that after my departing shall grievous wolves enter in among you, not
sparing the flock. 30Also of your own selves shall men arise, speaking
perverse things, to draw away disciples after them. 31Therefore watch,
and remember, that by the space of three years I ceased not to warn
every one night and day with tears.

8. **A genuine shepherd realized that he or they were placed in this exalted office by the Lord Himself, not by the church body.** This motivates him to shepherd God's way. **(Acts 20:28)**. Notice that the text does **not** say that the Holy Ghost made the flock overseers. The very fact that sheep without a shepherd would be scattered until they die or be killed, the very fact that sheep don't have enough sense, left to

themselves, should alert us to the fact that they have **no business** trying to shepherd the shepherd, just be sheep and be led. Why? Because God's sheep follow the shepherd's voice, goats do not.

9. **A true shepherd will <u>feed</u> the flock of God.** The sheep feed on the milk and the meat of the word of God. The responsibility of leadership is to take the word of God and teach the people. The flock's responsibility is to listen and **obey** it. The responsibility of leadership is to teach this bible in such a way that the **sense** of it is **clearly** proclaimed to the people of God.

Nehemiah 8:1-8, 13

1 And all the people gathered themselves together as one man into the street that [was] before the water gate; and they spake unto Ezra the scribe to bring the book of the law of Moses, which the LORD had commanded to Israel.

2 And Ezra the priest brought the law before the congregation both of men and women, and all that could hear with understanding, upon the first day of the seventh month.

3 And he read therein before the street that [was] before the water gate from the morning until midday, before the men and the women, and those that could understand; and the ears of all the people [were attentive] unto the book of the law.

4 And Ezra the scribe stood upon a pulpit of wood, which they had made for the purpose; and beside him stood Mattithiah, and Shema, and Anaiah, and Urijah, and Hilkiah, and Maaseiah, on his right hand; and on his left hand, Pedaiah, and Mishael, and Malchiah, and Hashum, and Hashbadana, Zechariah, [and] Meshullam.

5 And Ezra opened the book in the sight of all the people; (for he was above all the people;) and when he opened it, all the people stood up:

6 And Ezra blessed the LORD, the great God. And all the people answered, Amen, Amen, with lifting up their hands: and they bowed their heads, and worshipped the LORD with [their] faces to the ground.

7 Also Jeshua, and Bani, and Sherebiah, Jamin, Akkub, Shabbethai, Hodijah, Maaseiah, Kelita, Azariah, Jozabad, Hanan, Pelaiah, and the Levites, caused the people to understand the law: and the people [stood] in their place.

8 So they read in the book in the law of God distinctly, and gave the sense, and caused [them] to understand the reading.

13 And on the second day were gathered together the chief of the fathers of all the people, the priests, and the Levites, unto Ezra the scribe, even to understand the words of the law.

So we can see that there is a great need to teach God's people the word of God and that is the responsibility of leadership to do it, and God's leaders will do it! Hirelings don't!

But **this** is what usually happens in many churches today.

Ezekiel 33:30-33.

30 Also, thou son of man, the children of thy people still are talking against thee by the walls and in the doors of the houses, and

speak one to another, every one to his brother, saying, Come, I pray you, and hear what is the word that cometh forth from the LORD.

31 And they come unto thee as the people cometh, and they sit before thee [as] my people, and they hear thy words, but they will not do them: for with their mouth they shew much love, [but] their heart goeth after their covetousness.

32 And, lo, thou [art] unto them as a very lovely song of one that hath a pleasant voice, and can play well on an instrument: for they hear thy words, but they do them not.

10. **A true shepherd realizes that the price is <u>too great</u> for him, not to do his best in shepherding God's flock. (Acts 20:28)**. Christ died so that we may have this privilege to shepherd His people.

Acts 20:28

Take heed therefore unto yourselves, and to all the flock, over the which the Holy Ghost hath made you overseers, to feed the church of God, which he hath purchased with his own blood.

11. **A true shepherd had better <u>know</u> his enemies and the enemies of the flock. (Acts 20:29-30).** Don't be ignorant of God's word concerning the enemies of His people.

Acts 20:29-30

For I know this, that after my departing shall grievous wolves enter in among you, not sparing the flock. 30Also of your own selves shall men arise, speaking perverse things, to draw away disciples after them.

12. **A true shepherd is <u>always</u> on watch for the flock. (Acts 20:31).**

Acts 20:31

Therefore watch, and remember, that by the space of three years I ceased not to warn every one night and day with tears.

I Peter 5:2-4.

Feed the flock of God which is among you, taking the oversight *thereof,* not by constraint, but willingly; not for filthy lucre, but of a ready mind; 3Neither as being lords over *God's* heritage, but being ensamples to the flock. 4And when the chief Shepherd shall appear, ye shall receive a crown of glory that fadeth not away.

13. **A true shepherd will do his mission voluntarily and willingly. (I Peter 5:2).**

1 Peter 5:2

Feed the flock of God which is among you, taking the oversight *thereof,* not by constraint, but willingly; not for filthy lucre, but of a ready mind;

14. **A true shepherd will not make *<u>slaves</u>* out of the sheep. (I Peter 5:3).**

1 Peter 5:3

Neither as being lords over *God's* heritage, but being ensamples to the flock.

Shepherds will not overpower the sheep, will not master the sheep. The sheep and the shepherd share in a mutual and intimate relationship. This means that the sheep and the shepherd love each other and do exactly what the Lord says. There need not be any needless Lordship over **obedient sheep**.

15. True shepherds may never receive the respect, love and adoration they deserve, but they will be rewarded if they are faithful to God. (I Peter 5:4).

1 Peter 5:4

And when the chief Shepherd shall appear, ye shall receive a crown of glory that fadeth not away.

Caring about people is a responsibility of all Christians. Whether we are clergy or laity we can share God's love with the sick. Scripture tells of many times when God showed love. Jesus showed caring when he healed the sick. He healed the lame and restored sight to the blind. All are important to God and so should be important to us.

There are many in the pews who are hurting. There are people suffering physically, emotionally and mentally. As Christians we are called to care for those hurting. Some in the flock will have the gift of mercy, some empathy, some encouragement, some works. All in the congregation can help those in need. The shepherd who is wise will use all those in the flock to do God's work. Those who have the gift of helps can plan meals for the family to take some of the strain off the family. Those with the gift of encouragement can write encouraging notes to lift the spirits of the sick. Those with the gifts of mercy and empathy can sit with the patient and listen, offering comfort and compassion.

1 Peter 4:10-11

As every man hath received the gift, *even so* minister the same
one to another, as good stewards of the manifold grace of God. 11 If
any man speak, *let him speak* as the oracles of God; if any man
minister, *let him do it* as of the ability which God giveth: that God in
all things may be glorified through Jesus Christ, to whom be praise
and dominion for ever and ever. Amen.

CHAPTER TWO

JESUS' MINISTRY TO THE SICK

Jesus was a Healer while He walked on earth. He recognized the needs and vulnerability of the sick. His touch said to the people that He cared and they were worthwhile. Jesus restored many who were considered outcasts to the community.

Jesus Heals the Man with Leprosy

Matthew 8:1-4

When he was come down from the mountain, great multitudes followed him. [2] And, behold, there came a leper and worshipped him, saying, Lord, if thou wilt, thou canst make me clean. [3] And Jesus put forth his hand, and touched him, saying, I will; be thou clean. And immediately his leprosy was cleansed. [4] And Jesus saith unto him, See thou tell no man; but go thy way, shew thyself to the priest, and offer the gift that Moses commanded, for a testimony unto them.

Mark 1:40-45

And there came a leper to him, beseeching him, and kneeling down to him, and saying unto him, If thou wilt, thou canst make me clean. [41] And Jesus, moved with compassion, put forth his hand,

and touched him, and saith unto him, I will; be thou clean. [42] And as soon as he had spoken, immediately the leprosy departed from him, and he was cleansed. [43] And he straitly charged him, and forthwith sent him away; [44] And saith unto him, See thou say nothing to any man: but go thy way, shew thyself to the priest, and offer for thy cleansing those things which Moses commanded, for a testimony unto them. [45] But he went out, and began to publish it much, and to blaze abroad the matter, insomuch that Jesus could no more openly enter into the city, but was without in desert places: and they came to him from every quarter.

Luke 5:12-14

And it came to pass, when he was in a certain city, behold a man full of leprosy: who seeing Jesus fell on his face, and besought him, saying, Lord, if thou wilt, thou canst make me clean. [13] And he put forth his hand, and touched him, saying, I will: be thou clean. And immediately the leprosy departed from him. [14] And he charged him to tell no man: but go, and shew thyself to the priest, and offer for thy cleansing, according as Moses commanded, for a testimony unto them.

(8:1-4) **Leprosy**: William Barclay points out that leprosy was the most terrible disease in the day of Jesus, greatly feared. It was disfiguring and sometimes fatal. In the Bible leprosy is a type of sin (*The Gospel of Matthew*, Vol.1, p.300).

1. The leper himself was considered *utterly unclean*—physically and spiritually. He could not approach within six feet of any person including family members. "His clothes shall be rent, and his head bare, and he shall put a covering upon his upper lip, and shall cry, 'Unclean, unclean' " (Leviticus 13:45).

2. He was judged *dead*—the living dead. He had to wear a black garment so he could be recognized as being among the *dead.*

3. He was banished as an outcast, totally ostracized from society—earthly and heavenly. "All the days wherein the plague shall be in him he shall be defiled; he is unclean; he shall dwell alone; without the camp shall his habitation be" (Leviticus 13:46). He could not live within the walls of any city; his dwelling had to be outside the city gates.

4. He was thought to be polluted, incurable by any human means whatsoever. He could be cured by God and His power alone. (Note how Jesus proved His Messiahship and deity by healing the leper.)

Imagine the anguish and heartbreak of the leper, being completely cut off from family and friends and society. Imagine the emotional and mental pain. There are other recorded instances of lepers being healed (cp. Matthew 10:8; Matthew 11:5; Mark 1:40; Luke 7:22; Luke 17:12; and perhaps Matthew 26:6; cp. Mark 14:3).[1]

This leper was considered a defiled, unclean person. He was an outcast and considered polluted and incurable. Yet, the leper worshipped Jesus. He shows reverence by bowing before Jesus. Imagine his desperation. He was considered incurable and not allowed to pass within six feet of another person. This leper demonstrated that he acknowledged Jesus as being worthy of his praise and worship and he demonstrated that he was willing to break away from restrictions in seeking Christ. The leper asked and trusted Christ for cleansing. He wanted to be healed and restored.

The leper asked saying, "if thou wilt." This showed that the leper had faith in Jesus. He knew Jesus could heal him if He so chose. He was appealing to Jesus' heart and compassion. The appeal was not to His power; he showed that he knew Jesus had the power. He was asking for the love of Jesus to cleanse him.

---

[1] **Preachers Outline and Sermon Bible.** Leadership Ministries Worldwide.

John 11:22

But I know, that even now, whatsoever thou wilt ask of God, God will give it thee.

The leper came to Christ because he genuinely trusted and believed in Him and His power. He offered himself by bowing down to Christ and receiving His love.

Jesus' reaction to the leper was that of being deeply touched. He reached out to the man who was an outcast. The Lord touched the man whose body was covered with sores and whose flesh had been eaten away. He did not turn from the defiled. He "put forth His hand" to touch the man that no one else would touch.

This passage speaks loudly to my heart. There are many in our society who are cast out because of disease. Those with AIDS are treated like the lepers of Biblical times. Jesus showed by reaching out to the leper that, as Christians, we are to reach out to the defiled, unclean, outcasts. We are to show compassion to those in need.

John 20:21

Then said Jesus to them again, Peace be unto you: as my Father hath sent me, even so send I you.

Jesus warned the leper against pride in telling him to tell no one about what had happened. He wanted the man restored to his family and community so he sent him to obey the law in seeing the priests. If the priests said he was cured then he would be reunited with his family and friends.

The Faith of the Centurion

Matthew 8:5-13

And when Jesus was entered into Capernaum, there came unto him a centurion, beseeching him, [6] And saying, Lord, my servant lieth at home sick of the palsy, grievously tormented. [7] And Jesus saith unto him, I will come and heal him. [8] The centurion answered and said, Lord, I am not worthy that thou shouldest come under my roof: but speak the word only, and my servant shall be healed. [9] For I am a man under authority, having soldiers under me: and I say to this man, Go, and he goeth; and to another, Come, and he cometh; and to my servant, Do this, and he doeth it. [10] When Jesus heard it, he marvelled, and said to them that followed, Verily I say unto you, I have not found so great faith, no, not in Israel. [11] And I say unto you, That many shall come from the east and west, and shall sit down with Abraham, and Isaac, and Jacob, in the kingdom of heaven. [12] But the children of the kingdom shall be cast out into outer darkness: there shall be weeping and gnashing of teeth. [13] And Jesus said unto the centurion, Go thy way; and as thou hast believed, so be it done unto thee. And his servant was healed in the selfsame hour.

Luke 7:1-10

Now when he had ended all his sayings in the audience of the people, he entered into Capernaum. [2] And a certain centurion's servant, who was dear unto him, was sick, and ready to die. [3] And when he heard of Jesus, he sent unto him the elders of the Jews, beseeching him that he would come and heal his servant. [4] And when they came to Jesus, they besought him instantly, saying, That he was worthy for whom he should do this: [5] For he loveth our nation, and he hath built us a synagogue. [6] Then Jesus went with them. And when he was now not far from the house, the centurion sent friends to him, saying unto him, Lord, trouble not thyself: for I am not worthy that thou shouldest enter under my roof: [7] Wherefore neither thought I myself worthy to come unto thee: but say in a word, and my servant shall be healed. [8] For I also am a man set under authority, having under me soldiers, and I say unto one, Go, and he goeth; and to another, Come, and he cometh; and to my servant, Do this, and he doeth it. [9] When Jesus heard these things, he marvelled at him, and turned him about, and said unto the people that followed him, I say unto you, I have not found so great faith, no, not in Israel. [10] And they that were sent, returning to the house, found the servant whole that had been sick.

This passage about the Centurion's servant shows Jesus' Messianic power to heal. Jesus can heal anyone, regardless of the barrier.[2]

---

[2] **Preachers Outline and Sermon Bible.** Leadership Ministries Worldwide.

- The idealogical barrier: the centurion was hated by the Jews, yet Jesus could meet his need. He could overcome the ideas and prejudices that divided men.

- The physical barrier: the centurion's servant was very ill and many miles away. Jesus' power spanned the distance to heal the servant.

- The spiritual barrier: The centurion was a gentile, considered by the Jews to be lost spiritually and an enemy to God. Jesus had the power to pierce the spiritual barrier and save him. Jesus can reach the soul of any any man who will believe in Him, no matter how lost or how alien or how much of an enemy he has been.

The great faith of the centurion aroused Jesus to show his power as Messiah.

- Jesus' great power was aroused to receive the rejected. (v. 5-9)
- Jesus' great power was aroused to embrace all nationalities (v. 10-11).

- Jesus' great power was aroused to reject the unbelieving (v. 12).
- Jesus' great power proved His Messiahship. (v. 13)

In receiving the rejected, Jesus' power was aroused by the centurion's humility. He was a Gentile and a Roman officer, yet he came to a Jew for help. This was unheard of for a Roman officer to approach a Jew. This act showed Jesus that the centurion had great courage and humility. He approached Jesus as "Lord," acknowledging Him as His superior and Messiah. He knew and confessed that he had a need. These are two essential things in having needs met. The centurion knew where to go to have his need met. He trusted Jesus to meet this need.

Jesus' response to the cry for help was "I will." This meant that Jesus would overcome all the barriers previously listed. Jesus will meet the need of anyone who truly trusts Him. Jesus does not have favorites; He loves everyone.

Acts 10:34-35

Then Peter opened his mouth, and said, "Of a truth I perceive that God is no respecter of persons: [35] But in every nation he that feareth him, and worketh righteousness, is accepted with him."

Romans 10:12

For there is no difference between the Jew and the Greek: for the same Lord over all is rich unto all that call upon him.

Jesus' power was aroused by the personal sense of unworthiness on the part of the centurion. He confessed his inadequacy and unworthiness to have the Lord help him.

Matthew 23:12

And whosoever shall exalt himself shall be abased; and he that shall humble himself shall be exalted.

James 4:6

But he giveth more grace. Wherefore he saith, God resisteth the proud, but giveth grace unto the humble.

James 4:10

Humble yourselves in the sight of the Lord, and he shall lift you up.

Psalm 138:6

Though the Lord be high, yet hath he respect unto the lowly: but the proud he knoweth afar off.

Jesus' power was aroused by the centurion's love for his servant. The centurion was pouring out his heart for someone else (intercessory prayer). The centurion loved this man who was lower socially. This should be a lesson to us that we are to love all, regardless of what others may think. As believers, we are to love. We aren't just to love those close to us; or those easy to love; we are to love all. This means we are to love those who are sick, those who are outcast because of deforming diseases.

Jesus' power was aroused by the centurion's great faith. The faith the centurion displayed was a personal faith. He had faith that Jesus could overcome the barriers and heal his servant. He had faith in Jesus as Lord.

How does this story relate to our ministry to the sick? Jesus still overcomes all barriers. He listens to our intercessory prayers. Jesus loves everyone. He looks not at the station in life, but at the condition of the heart. We are to go about the ministry of caring for the sick by visiting and praying for all. I believe this passage also teaches that as Christians, we are to love and show love to those who are in need. Pastors not only need to show God's love, but also need to show compassion and love on their own part.

Jesus Heals Peter's Mother-in-law

Matthew 8:14-17

And when Jesus was come into Peter's house, he saw his wife's mother laid, and sick of a fever. [15] And he touched her hand, and the fever left her: and she arose, and ministered unto them.

[16] When the even was come, they brought unto him many that were possessed with devils: and he cast out the spirits with his word, and healed all that were sick: [17] That it might be fulfilled which was

spoken by Esaias (Isaiah) the prophet, saying, Himself took our infirmities, and bare our sicknesses.

Mark 1:29-34

And forthwith, when they were come out of the synagogue, they entered into the house of Simon and Andrew, with James and John. [30] But Simon's wife's mother lay sick of a fever, and anon they tell him of her. [31] And he came and took her by the hand, and lifted her up; and immediately the fever left her, and she ministered unto them. [32] And at even, when the sun did set, they brought unto him all that were diseased, and them that were possessed with devils. [33] And all the city was gathered together at the door. [34] And he healed many that were sick of divers diseases, and cast out many devils; and suffered not the devils to speak, because they knew him.

Luke 4:38-41

And he arose out of the synagogue, and entered into Simon's house. And Simon's wife's mother was taken with a great fever; and they besought him for her. [39] And he stood over her, and rebuked the fever; and it left her: and immediately she arose and ministered unto them.

[40] Now when the sun was setting, all they that had any sick with divers diseases brought them unto him; and he laid his hands on every one of them, and healed them. [41] And devils also came out of many, crying out, and saying, Thou art Christ the Son of God. And he rebuking them suffered them not to speak: for they knew that he was Christ.

This passage on Jesus' healing Peter's mother-in-law teaches us about Jesus' power and its purpose. One of the purposes Jesus came to earth was to meet the needs of individuals and families. Jesus went to Peter's home to rest. He had been at the synagogue teaching and healing. On his way to Peter's house he stopped to heal the centurion's servant. He was very tired and needed to rest. Yet when He entered Peter's home he found yet another sick person, Peter's mother-in-law. This woman was an individual in a private home. Jesus would have no audience, no one to recognize the healing. But, Jesus had come to help individuals so He did just that; He helped the woman. He forgot about His own need and ministered to the woman.

Peter's mother-in-law represents the quiet and unknown of society. This woman was just as important to Jesus as any other. Her need got His attention. Jesus "touched" her. The act of touching shows great warmth and compassion. Many who are sick have not been tenderly and warmly touched. Jesus is giving us an example of how we can minister to the sick by communicating His love through touch. There is also a power when we touch and pray. This power is an infusion of assurance of real assurance and confidence over whatever is being prayed.

1 John 5:14-15

And this is the confidence that we have in him, that, if we ask any thing according to his will, he heareth us: [15] And if we know that he hear us, whatsoever we ask, we know that we have the petitions that we desired of him.

Ephes. 3:20

Now unto him that is able to do exceeding abundantly above all that we ask or think, according to the power that worketh in us,

Hebrews 4:15-16

For we have not an high priest which cannot be touched with the feeling of our infirmities; but was in all points tempted like as we are, yet without sin. [16] Let us therefore come boldly unto the throne of grace that we may obtain mercy, and find grace to help in time of need.

Peter's mother-in-law's reaction was to get up and immediately start serving the Lord. From this we learn that when Jesus touches us, we need to get up immediately and begin serving. When Jesus touches us with His power it is for service, not self-importance. We are not to wait for others to start serving; we are to get busy ourselves in the ministry of the Lord.

This passage not only speaks of the Lord healing individuals but it also speaks of His healing the multitudes. Remember, Jesus was very tired and had gone to Peter's house to rest. But, the multitudes came to him to be healed. Jesus was on earth to help meet the needs of individuals and families. He didn't turn anyone away. This is a picture of how desperately the world needs Jesus. He came for the lost, the sick, and all who would come.

Luke 19:10

For the Son of man is come to seek and to save that which was lost.

Matthew 20:28

Even as the Son of man came not to be ministered unto, but to minister, and to give his life a ransom for many.

Matthew 11:28

Come unto me, all ye that labour and are heavy laden, and I will give you rest.

Jesus had enough power to help all. He could meet all needs.

Acts 10:38

How God anointed Jesus of Nazareth with the Holy Ghost and with power: who went about doing good, and healing all that were oppressed of the devil; for God was with him.

Jairus' daughter and the Hopeless Need.....A Woman with a Blood Issue

Matthew 9:18-26

While he spake these things unto them, behold, there came a certain ruler, and worshipped him, saying, My daughter is even now dead: but come and lay thy hand upon her, and she shall live. [19] And Jesus arose, and followed him, and so did his disciples.

[20] And, behold, a woman, which was diseased with an issue of blood twelve years, came behind him, and touched the hem of his garment: [21] For she said within herself, If I may but touch his garment, I shall be whole. [22] But Jesus turned him about, and when he saw her, he said, Daughter, be of good comfort; thy faith hath made thee whole. And the woman was made whole from that hour. [23] And when Jesus came into the ruler's house, and saw the minstrels and the people making a noise, [24] He said unto them, Give place: for the maid is not dead, but sleepeth. And they laughed him to scorn. [25] But when the people were put forth, he went in, and took her by the hand, and the maid arose. [26] And the fame hereof went abroad into all that land.

Mark 5:21-43

And when Jesus was passed over again by ship unto the other side, much people gathered unto him: and he was nigh unto the sea. [22] And, behold, there cometh one of the rulers of the synagogue, Jairus by name; and when he saw him, he fell at his feet, [23] And besought him greatly, saying, My little daughter lieth at the point of death: I pray thee, come and lay thy hands on her, that she may be healed; and she shall live. [24] And Jesus went with him; and much people followed him, and thronged him. [25] And a certain woman, which had an issue of blood twelve years, [26] And had suffered many things of many physicians, and had spent all that she had, and was nothing bettered, but rather grew worse, [27] When she had heard of Jesus, came in the press behind, and touched his garment. [28] For she said, If I may touch but his clothes, I shall be whole. [29] And straightway the fountain of her blood was dried up; and she felt in her body that she was healed of that plague. [30] And Jesus, immediately knowing in himself that virtue had gone out of him, turned him about in the press, and said, Who touched my clothes? [31] And his disciples said unto him, Thou seest the multitude thronging thee, and sayest thou, Who touched me? [32] And he looked round about to see her that had done this thing. [33] But the woman fearing and trembling, knowing what was done in her, came and fell down before him, and told him all the truth. [34] And he said unto her, Daughter, thy faith hath made thee whole; go in peace, and be whole of thy plague. [35] While he yet spake, there came from the ruler of the synagogue's house certain which said, Thy daughter is dead: why troublest thou the Master any further? [36] As soon as Jesus heard the word that was spoken, he saith unto the ruler of the synagogue, Be not afraid, only believe. [37] And he suffered no man to follow him, save Peter, and James, and John the brother of James. [38] And he cometh to the house of the ruler of the synagogue, and seeth the tumult, and them that wept and wailed greatly. [39] And when he was come in, he saith unto them, Why make ye this ado, and weep? the damsel is not dead, but sleepeth. [40] And they laughed him to scorn. But when he had put them all out, he taketh the father and the mother of the damsel, and them that were with him, and entereth in where the damsel was lying. [41] And he took the damsel by the hand, and said unto her, Talitha cumi; which is, being interpreted, Damsel, I say unto thee, arise. [42] And straightway the damsel arose, and walked; for she was of the age of twelve years. And they were astonished with a great astonishment. [43] And he charged them straitly that no man should know it; and commanded that something should be given her to eat.

Luke 8:40-56

And it came to pass, that, when Jesus was returned, the people gladly received him: for they were all waiting for him.

[41] And, behold, there came a man named Jairus, and he was a ruler of the synagogue: and he fell down at Jesus' feet, and besought him that he would come into his house: [42] For he had one only daughter, about twelve years of age, and she lay a dying. But as he went the people thronged him.

[43] And a woman having an issue of blood twelve years, which had spent all her living upon physicians, neither could be healed of any, [44] Came behind him, and touched the border of his garment: and immediately her issue of blood stanched. [45] And Jesus said, Who touched me? When all denied, Peter and they that were with him said, Master, the multitude throng thee and press thee, and sayest thou, Who touched me? [46] And Jesus said, Somebody hath touched me: for I perceive that virtue is gone out of me. [47] And when the

woman saw that she was not hid, she came trembling, and falling down before him, she declared unto him before all the people for what cause she had touched him and how she was healed immediately. [48] And he said unto her, Daughter, be of good comfort: thy faith hath made thee whole; go in peace.

[49] While he yet spake, there cometh one from the ruler of the synagogue's house, saying to him, Thy daughter is dead; trouble not the Master. [50] But when Jesus heard it, he answered him, saying, Fear not: believe only, and she shall be made whole. [51] And when he came into the house, he suffered no man to go in, save Peter, and James, and John, and the father and the mother of the maiden. [52] And all wept, and bewailed her: but he said, Weep not; she is not dead, but sleepeth. [53] And they laughed him to scorn, knowing that she was dead. [54] And he put them all out, and took her by the hand, and called, saying, Maid, arise. [55] And her spirit came again, and she arose straightway: and he commanded to give her meat. [56] And her parents were astonished: but he charged them that they should tell no man what was done.

The Preacher's Outline and Sermon Bible gives a wonderful commentary on this passage. Note here that there was a hopeless cry for life. The man who cried for help was a ruler and a father. Luke says that the ruler's name who oversaw the administration of the synagogue at Capernaum was Jairus. He was an elected ruler and highly respected. He held great power. He was one of the most important men in the community.

He was so hopeless that he interrupted Jesus while He was preaching and teaching. His daughter was dead. He loved his daughter deeply. He stood up against the hostility of his peers to approach Jesus. Jesus responded to the cries of a helpless, hopeless man by stopping what He was doing, and rising up to go with the man.

That is a model for us to follow. When a need arises, we too are to rise up and go. If someone is in an accident and you are called at 2 AM you are to rise up and go. It should have priority over all else when there is a need and you arc called upon to go.

Look at the attitude of Jairus. He fell down at Jesus' feet and worshipped Him. This man was a distinguished, elected man who held a high position, yet he approached the Lord with humility, worship and faith.

Matthew 18:4

Whosoever therefore shall humble himself as this little child, the same is greatest in the kingdom of heaven.

James 4:6

But he giveth more grace. Wherefore he saith, God resisteth the proud, but giveth grace unto the humble.

James 4:10

Humble yourselves in the sight of the Lord, and he shall lift you up.

Often when people are driven into helplessness and hopelessness they go to a state of depression and self-pity. The need may be severe illness, terrible trouble, or death. Despair is not the answer to desperate needs. The answer is to bow down before the Lord and ask Him for help.

Jairus asked Jesus to go and touch his daughter. He asked Jesus to touch his need.

Psalm 91:15

He shall call upon me, and I will answer him: I will be with him in trouble; I will deliver him, and honour him.

Isaiah 58:9

Then shalt thou call, and the Lord shall answer; thou shalt cry, and he shall say, Here I am. If thou take away from the midst of thee the yoke, the putting forth of the finger, and speaking vanity;

Jeremiah 33:3

Call unto me, and I will answer thee, and shew thee great and mighty things, which thou knowest not.

Jairus asked Jesus to put His hands on her so she would live. This is a show of great faith. He believed that if Jesus would just go and touch his dead daughter that she would raise from the dead.

We need this kind of faith also. We need to have faith that Jesus will meet needs. This man was driven to Jesus by a tragedy. I have learned through my experiences that those in situations where there is illness or tragedy that people either draw closer to the Lord or turn and run away. As pastors and spiritual care givers, it is our calling to guide people to a closer relationship with the Lord. We can show them how to approach the Lord with a spirit of worship and belief, and trusting that Jesus will hear our prayers and help.

Matthew 21:22

And all things, whatsoever ye shall ask in prayer, believing, ye shall receive.

John 14:14

If ye shall ask any thing in my name, I will do it.

Psalm 91:15

He shall call upon me, and I will answer him: I will be with him in trouble; I will deliver him, and honour him.

Jesus responded to the father's desperation by following the man and going where He was needed without hesitation.

Jeremiah 33:3

Call unto me, and I will answer thee, and shew thee great and mighty things, which thou knowest not.

Jesus responds to the cries of the hopeless and desperate. He never turns from anyone who comes to Him for help. Jesus will come to us wherever our need is. Jesus placed a high priority on helping someone in need.

On the way to Jairus' house, Jesus was stopped by a woman with an issue of bleeding. She had been hemorrhaging for 12 years. She felt hopeless, ashamed, embarrassed and unworthy. According to the law she was to be isolated. She should not have been in the crowd surrounding Jesus at all. But she was desperate and knew that if she could just touch Jesus' cloak she would be healed. He knew when she touched His robe. He knew because her faith had touched Him.

Mark 9:23

Jesus said unto him, If thou canst believe, all things are possible to him that believeth.

Psalm 37:5

Commit thy way unto the Lord; trust also in him; and he shall bring it to pass.

Jesus infuses all those who place faith in Him with His virtue. She was infused with His power and life.

Mark 5:30

And Jesus, immediately knowing in himself that virtue had gone out of him, turned him about in the press, and said, Who touched my clothes?

Jesus saw the woman and her desperation. He saw her need and His heart went out to her. Jesus cares for all no matter how unclean they are. We are all precious to Him.

Hebrews 4:15-16

For we have not an high priest which cannot be touched with the feeling of our infirmities; but was in all points tempted like as we are, yet without sin. [16] Let us therefore come boldly unto the throne of grace, that we may obtain mercy, and find grace to help in time of need.

Jesus adopted the woman. He called her "daughter" and adopted her into the family of God. He spoke to her on behalf of the Father and gave her the assurance that she was accepted by God. When we go to God in desperation, He gives us a release from pressure and desperation and a knowledge of adoption and comfort. [3]

John 1:12

[3] **Preacher's Outline and Sermon Bible.** Leadership Ministries Worldwide.

But as many as received him, to them gave he power to become the sons of God, even to them that believe on his name:

Romans 8:15

For ye have not received the spirit of bondage again to fear; but ye have received the Spirit of adoption, whereby we cry, Abba, Father.

2 Cor. 6:18

And will be a Father unto you, and ye shall be my sons and daughters, saith the Lord Almighty.

Scripture again picks up the story about Jairus' daughter. It is interesting that the story of the woman with the issue of blood was inserted in the middle. Surely Jairus became a bit nervous when Jesus was delayed. Or, could he possibly have been strengthened by seeing Jesus heal the woman by faith? God's timing is always perfect, so there was a reason for the delay.

Jesus cleared the room of noise and commotion. Jesus wants us to go to Him in quiet, prayerful meditation. Noises of the earth have no hope of conquering sickness or death. The Lord works in quiet ways. He gives quiet assurance and hope to those who trust in Him. We cannot feel His comfort if we are in the midst of noise.

The mourners scorned Jesus. Men scoffed at the idea of Jesus raising Jairus' daughter from the dead. Jairus, however, trusted in the Lord. Jesus went in to the girl. He will always "go in" when the door is open and He is welcomed. When He took her by the hand, He infused her with his power and life. He raised her up. Jesus again proved that He was the Messiah by raising the girl from the dead.

Jesus Heals the Blind and Mute

Matthew 9:27-31

And when Jesus departed thence, two blind men followed him, crying, and saying, Thou Son of David, have mercy on us. [28] And when he was come into the house, the blind men came to him: and Jesus saith unto them, Believe ye that I am able to do this? They said unto him, Yea, Lord. [29] Then touched he their eyes, saying, According to your faith be it unto you. [30] And their eyes were opened; and Jesus straitly charged them, saying, See that no man know it. [31] But they, when they were departed, spread abroad his fame in all that country.

Matthew 20:29-34

And as they departed from Jericho, a great multitude followed him.

[30] And, behold, two blind men sitting by the way side, when they heard that Jesus passed by, cried out, saying, Have mercy on us, O Lord, thou Son of David. [31] And the multitude rebuked them, because they should hold their peace: but they cried the more, saying, Have mercy on us, O Lord, thou Son of David. [32] And Jesus stood still, and called them, and said, What will ye that I shall do unto you? [33] They say unto him, Lord, that our eyes may be opened. [34] So Jesus had compassion on them, and touched their eyes: and immediately their eyes received sight, and they followed him.

There was an unceasing cry for sight from two blind men. The blind men had been sitting beside the road begging, as the blind did in Jesus' day. They overheard what had been happening so they followed Jesus crying out, "Thou Son of David, Have mercy on us."

These men acknowledged that Jesus was the Messiah, the Savior of the world. This is seen in the title they used, "Thou Son of David." They cried for mercy. This must be done if we want God to have mercy on us. These men believed by faith. They couldn't see what was happening around them. They could only hear the reports. Yet, they believed and cried out for mercy, confessing Christ as the Messiah.

Psalm 34:6

This poor man cried, and the Lord heard him, and saved him out of all his troubles.

Psalm 34:18

The Lord is nigh unto them that are of a broken heart; and saveth such as be of a contrite spirit.

God is merciful. He will have mercy on those who cry out to Him. These men were persistent. They followed Jesus crying out to Him for mercy. Jesus was not angry with their persistence. He knew they were genuine.

Matthew 7:8

For every one that asketh receiveth; and he that seeketh findeth; and to him that knocketh it shall be opened.

Deut. 4:29

But if from thence thou shalt seek the Lord thy God, thou shalt find him, if thou seek him with all thy heart and with all thy soul.

Jeremiah 29:13

And ye shall seek me, and find me, when ye shall search for me with all your heart.

These men sought the Lord. They asked Him to have mercy on them. They were persistent in their faith. Jesus responded with compassion. Jesus asked of the men, “Believe ye that I am able to do this?” Jesus wanted the men to respond from their hearts, what He knew was there, that He could heal them.

Hebrews 11:6

But without faith it is impossible to please him: for he that cometh to God must believe that he is, and that he is a rewarder of them that diligently seek him.

Proverbs 3:5

Trust in the Lord with all thine heart; and lean not unto thine own understanding.

Jesus met their need. He exerted His power and healed them, based on their faith. It took faith to bring about their healing. Jesus knows our heart. He knows our faith. He knows when we need a trial to bring about a stronger faith.

Matthew 21:22

And all things, whatsoever ye shall ask in prayer, believing, ye shall receive.

Hebrews 11:6

But without faith it is impossible to please him: for he that cometh to God must believe that he is, and that he is a rewarder of them that diligently seek him.

Christ sent these men away with their sight restored.

The Workers are Few

Matthew 9:35-38

And Jesus went about all the cities and villages, teaching in their synagogues, and preaching the gospel of the kingdom, and healing every sickness and every disease among the people.

[36] But when he saw the multitudes, he was moved with compassion on them, because they fainted, and were scattered abroad, as sheep having no shepherd. [37] Then saith he unto his disciples, The harvest truly is plenteous, but the labourers are few; [38] Pray ye therefore the Lord of the harvest, that he will send forth labourers into his harvest.

This passage of scripture gives us the threefold mission of Christ. Christ came to minister, to demonstrate His compassion, and to tell men the good news.

Christ came to minister. Jesus' method of reaching people was to go out to the villages and into the cities. He went to the people. He didn't sit back and wait for the people to come to Him.

Luke 19:10

For the Son of man is come to seek and to save that which was lost.

Jesus went everywhere. He could be found in synagogues, on the countryside, in boats, in homes, or by the seashore.

Matthew 22:9

Go ye therefore into the highways, and as many as ye shall find, bid to the marriage.

Acts 1:8

But ye shall receive power, after that the Holy Ghost is come upon you: and ye shall be witnesses unto me both in Jerusalem, and in all Judaea, and in Samaria, and unto the uttermost part of the earth.

Jesus went about doing His work everywhere. He went into small villages and where the lower class lived. He went wherever there were people. He proclaimed the news of God and the message of salvation. He taught the people so they would be rooted and know how to live. Jesus also met the physical needs of those who were suffering.

Christ had a mission to show compassion. He was to express and demonstrate God's compassion, the kind of compassion all men are to have for all other men. Jesus "saw the multitudes." He saw those following Him-those in the villages, in the cities, in the countryside, in the synagogues, on the mountains, by the seashore, by the graveyards, in boats and in homes-and He "was moved with compassion." Jesus was moved over physical needs of men: their hunger, pain, and suffering. He was moved over the spiritual needs of men: their being lost and dead to God; their emptiness and loneliness and bewilderment; their having no purpose, meaning or significance in life. He saw them all and He observed and studied them.[4]

Jesus looked out upon the people and had compassion. He saw that they were weighed down by life, religion and sin. They were not being taught the truth. They were being deceived by their leaders. He saw the people as without a shepherd to lead them to God. Christ saw a world in need of workers for God. God calls men to reach the lost with the gospel. God also calls and gifts us to the mission field of compassion. He calls us to the beside of the child with cancer. He calls us to the bedside of the man with AIDS. He calls us to the bedside of the elderly who are nearing the end of life. He calls us to visit the sick regardless of what afflicts them and regardless of where they live.

Ephes. 4:11

And he gave some, apostles; and some, prophets; and some, evangelists; and some, pastors and teachers;

---

[4] **Preachers Outline and Sermon Bible.** Leadership Ministries Worldwide.

CHAPTER THREE

THE DISCIPLES HEAL

The Disciples Heal

Matthew 10:1

And when he had called unto him his twelve disciples, he gave them power against unclean spirits, to cast them out, and to heal all manner of sickness and all manner of disease.

Jesus gave the disciples the power to heal and sent them out. They healed many while following Jesus.

After Jesus left the earth, the disciples continued healing in Jesus' name. This was a sign that proved that Jesus is alive and that He is working through His disciples. God demonstrated His power through His followers.

Peter Heals the Crippled Beggar

Acts 3:1-11

Now Peter and John went up together into the temple at the hour of prayer, being the ninth hour. [2] And a certain man lame from his mother's womb was carried, whom they laid daily at the gate of the temple which is called Beautiful, to ask alms of them that entered into the temple; [3] Who seeing Peter and John about to go into the temple asked an alms. [4] And Peter, fastening his eyes upon him with John, said, Look on us. [5] And he gave heed unto them, expecting to receive something of them. [6] Then Peter said, Silver and gold have I none; but such as I have give I thee: In the name of Jesus Christ of Nazareth rise up and walk. [7] And he took him by the right hand, and lifted him up: and immediately his feet and ankle bones received strength. [8] And he leaping up stood, and walked, and entered with them into the temple, walking, and leaping, and praising God. [9] And all the people saw him walking and praising God: [10] And they knew that it was he which sat for alms at the Beautiful gate of the temple: and they were filled with wonder and amazement at that which had happened unto him. [11] And as the lame man which was healed held Peter and John, all the people ran together unto them in the porch that is called Solomon's, greatly wondering.

Jesus wants His followers to know that He is still present and still has power. He is still at work. Jesus works through those who are faithful in prayer. He works through those who look and see the desperate need of the suffering in spirit and body.

Peter and John were faithful in prayer. The phrase, "The ninth hour," means around three o'clock in the afternoon. The Jews observed three times daily for prayer. They prayed at the third hour (9 a.m.), the sixth hour (12 noon), and the ninth hour (3 p.m.).

Psalm 55:17

Evening, and morning, and at noon, will I pray, and cry aloud: and he shall hear my voice.

We know very little about the lame beggar. We know that he was lame from birth and since he was unable to work, he was placed at the temple gate to beg daily. We know that he was known by all in the community. This man was also hurting from within. He did not even look at those from whom he was begging. He had been this way his whole life. Many had passed by him, not noticing his need. Jesus works through those who fasten their eyes upon the needs. Peter and John fastened their eyes upon the lame man. They fixed their attention upon him. Peter would not look away, because he was indwelt by the Holy Spirit. Peter was there to do God's will in meeting the needs of the world. Peter was filled with compassion for the man.

Jesus was able to work through Peter because he reached out to meet the needs of the man. Peter knew the need, knew the Lord cared and acted as the Lord's representative. Peter told the lame man to, "Look on us." This stirred an expectancy within the man to receive something. By commanding the man to "Look upon them" he showed that he was sure he belonged to God, that he had a plan, that he expected that his faith in God would help him meet the need, and that he had a willingness to act.

The man expected to be helped by being given worldly things. He expected silver or gold. This wasn't what the man really needed. God saw the man's physical and spiritual need. Man's spiritual welfare is his basic need. God wanted to cure the whole man. By making the man whole, he will become productive and fulfill his purpose on earth.

Power and authority are found in Jesus' name. Peter called upon the name of Jesus. To call upon the name of someone means to call upon the authority and power of the person. When Peter said, "In the name of Jesus Christ of Nazareth, rise up and walk," he was proclaiming: "It is the name, the power, the authority, the Person of Jesus Christ who will heal you." Jesus is alive. His power, His authority, His name, and His Person are still active upon earth.[5]

It was not Peter that met the need. It was the name of the power of Jesus Christ that met the need. Christ alone, in power and presence, met the need. Peter knew that the power of Jesus dwelt within him. Peter knew that he possessed the power and presence of Christ. He knew that he was a called representative of Christ. Peter knew that his purpose was to represent Christ and to share Christ's power with those who are sick and hurting.

Peter reached down, took the man's hand and lifted him up. The man took Peter's hand. He trusted Peter. Jesus healed the lame man.

---

[5] **Preachers Outline and Sermon Bible.** Leadership Ministries Worldwide.

Peter had faith in Jesus' presence and power. The lame man trusted in Peter, opening the door for Jesus to heal.

Matthew 17:20

And Jesus said unto them, Because of your unbelief: for verily I say unto you, If ye have faith as a grain of mustard seed, ye shall say unto this mountain, Remove hence to yonder place; and it shall remove; and nothing shall be impossible unto you.

John 14:13

And whatsoever ye shall ask in my name, that will I do, that the Father may be glorified in the Son.

John 16:24

Hitherto have ye asked nothing in my name: ask, and ye shall receive, that your joy may be full.

Ephes. 3:20

Now unto him that is able to do exceeding abundantly above all that we ask or think, according to the power that worketh in us,

The results of the healing were that the people knew the man had truly been healed. They also knew there was no question of the miracle because the man had been lame since birth. They were filled with wonder and wanted to know what had caused the miracle. Others desired miracles in their lives.

Matthew 5:16

Let your light so shine before men, that they may see your good works, and glorify your Father which is in heaven.

Psalm 66:16

Come and hear, all ye that fear God, and I will declare what he hath done for my soul.

Isaiah 63:7

I will mention the lovingkindnesses of the Lord, and the praises of the Lord, according to all that the Lord hath bestowed on us, and the great goodness toward the house of Israel, which he hath bestowed on them according to his mercies, and according to the multitude of his lovingkindnesses.

The Healing of Aeneas

Acts 9:32-35

And it came to pass, as Peter passed throughout all quarters, he came down also to the saints which dwelt at Lydda. [33] And there he found a certain man named Aeneas, which had kept his bed eight years, and was sick of the palsy. [34] And Peter said unto him, Aeneas, Jesus Christ maketh thee whole: arise, and make thy bed. And he arose immediately. [35] And all that dwelt at Lydda and Saron saw him, and turned to the Lord.

Peter was a dedicated disciple. He was the called apostle to the Jews.

Galatians 2:8

(For he that wrought effectually in Peter to the apostleship of the circumcision, the same was mighty in me toward the Gentiles:)

The Jews were scattered throughout Palestine because of the persecution. Peter was called to reach out to Jewish believers wherever they were. Peter had visited Judea, Galilee. And Samaria. Peter faithfully fulfilled his calling. He preached to the lost and discipled the believers.

Peter went to Lydda. Lydda was located 30 miles northwest of Jerusalem and 10 miles south of Joppa. Lydda was an important commercial city. God chose the city of Lydda to demonstrate the power of Jesus. Many saints lived there.

Peter encountered a man who had been bedridden for eight years. The man was paralyzed, unable to walk or even get out of bed. The man had a desperate need to be healed. It seemed hopeless because there was no hope of recovery given. Aenas' future seemed to be doomed to his bed.

We really know nothing of Aenas other than he was paralyzed and bedridden for eight years. Since he was bedridden, he probably was not famous and probably contributed nothing to society. But, God still loved Aenas and would heal him.

Peter boldly told Aenas that "Jesus Christ maketh him whole, to arise and make his bed." It was the love, authority, and power of Jesus that healed Aenas. "Maketh whole" means to be healed immediately, here and now. He was healed inside and out. He was healed physically and spiritually. Peter commanded the man to believe by telling him to get up and make his bed. Aenas had to show that he believed that he had been healed by getting up.

Hebrews 11:6

But without faith it is impossible to please him: for he that cometh to God must believe that he is, and that he is a rewarder of them that diligently seek him.

The result was Aenas was healed. He got up immediately and walked. Others saw what Peter had done in Jesus' name. All who lived in Lydda and Sharon turned to the Lord. Seeing the power of Christ in Aenas' life turned others to Christ.

Conquering the Death of Dorcas

Acts 9:36-43

Now there was at Joppa a certain disciple named Tabitha, which by interpretation is called Dorcas: this woman was full of good works and almsdeeds which she did. [37] And it came to pass in those days, that she was sick, and died: whom when they had washed, they laid her in an upper chamber. [38] And forasmuch as Lydda was nigh to Joppa, and the disciples had heard that Peter was there, they sent unto him two men, desiring him that he would not delay to come to them. [39] Then Peter arose and went with them. When he was come, they brought him into the upper chamber: and all the widows stood by him weeping, and shewing the coats and garments which Dorcas made, while she was with them. [40] But Peter put them all forth, and kneeled down, and prayed; and turning him to the body said, Tabitha, arise. And she opened her eyes: and when she saw Peter, she sat up. [41] And he gave her his hand, and lifted her up, and when he had called the saints and widows, presented her alive. [42] And it was known throughout all Joppa; and many believed in the Lord. [43] And it came to pass, that he tarried many days in Joppa with one Simon a tanner.

Joppa was the seaport city for Jerusalem and the capital of Israel. It was the only seaport that could provide shelter between Egypt and Mt. Carmel. This busy seaport was inhabited by Jews and Gentiles. Joppa dates back to the time of Jonah. Joppa is also where Peter had the vision that led him to evangelize to the Gentiles.

The raising of Dorcas, or Tabitha in Hebrew, demonstrates the disciples being able to raise the dead through the power of Jesus. Dorcas was a faithful believer who was deeply committed to Christ. She was "full of good works," meaning she served and did all kinds of good to all who needed help. "Almsdeeds which she did," refers to the giving of gifts, which she made. Dorcas must have had wealth because she purchased material to make clothing for poor widows. Dorcas was faithful in serving.[6]

---

[6] ***Preacher's Outline and Sermon Bible.*** Leadership Ministries Worldwide.

Matthew 5:16

Let your light so shine before men, that they may see your good works, and glorify your Father which is in heaven.

2 Cor. 8:11

Now therefore perform the doing of it; that as there was a readiness to will, so there may be a performance also out of that which ye have.

2 Cor. 9:7

Every man according as he purposeth in his heart, so let him give; not grudgingly, or of necessity: for God loveth a cheerful giver.

Titus 2:7

In all things shewing thyself a pattern of good works: in doctrine shewing uncorruptness, gravity, sincerity,

Hebrews 10:24

And let us consider one another to provoke unto love and to good works:

Dorcas tragically died in the midst of her ministry. The believers were crushed, believing that the ministry could not continue without Dorcas. The believers in Joppa were apparently newer converts who had not yet matured in Christ. Apparently, there were many poor people in Joppa and no one had the finances to continue this ministry.

Word had spread about the disciples and how Peter had healed, through Jesus, the paralytic in Lydda. They also knew that Jesus could raise the dead. They knew that Peter was close and that if he would come, he could call upon Jesus to raise Dorcas from the dead.

It was the custom of the Jew to bury the dead soon after death. But, instead of burying Dorcas they washed her and placed her in the upper room. They sent two men to bring Peter to Joppa to seek out the Lord in raising Dorcas. These acts showed great faith. The men asked Peter to "delay not" in coming to Joppa. They did not want him to hesitate, but to come quickly without questioning. Peter acted as a loving pastor in his response. He knew the need and heard the deep sorrow felt by the believers.

Peter did not have the power to raise the dead. The power came from Jesus. Peter could raise the dead in the power of the name of Jesus Christ. **Peter sent everyone out of the room and prayed to the living Lord.** He asked for the Lord's will. Remember, it is not always God's will to heal physically. When God listens to our requests, He considers four things. He considers His glory. Would granting the request bring the greatest glory to God's name? He considers our good, not only physically, but spiritually. What do we need to learn? Will granting our request strengthen us more spiritually? How does God now want to use us? God knows what is needed and by whom; when it is needed; for whom it is needed; where it is needed; how it is needed; and why it is needed. God also considers mercy. He wills above all else for men to know His mercy. He does whatever is needed to demonstrate His mercy to men. Sometimes His mercy is revealed more through walking through the trials of life, sometimes His mercy is revealed more when the trials are removed. Clearly, Jesus Christ has the power to heal the believer who needs to be healed. The need for healing is not always the greatest need of the person. God sometimes uses physical need to meet the spiritual need of a believer. Sometimes the believer needs to learn through suffering.[7]

James 1:2-4

My brethren, count it all joy when ye fall into divers temptations; [3] Knowing this, that the trying of your faith worketh patience. [4] But let patience have her perfect work, that ye may be perfect and entire, wanting nothing.

James 1:12

Blessed is the man that endureth temptation: for when he is tried, he shall receive the crown of life, which the Lord hath promised to them that love him.

When Peter knew that the Lord wanted Dorcas raised, he prayed for the power to raise her and for God to use the miracle to make men believe.

Acts 9:42

---

[7] Ibid.

And it was known throughout all Joppa; and many believed in the Lord.

Matthew 6:6

But thou, when thou prayest, enter into thy closet, and when thou hast shut thy door, pray to thy Father which is in secret; and thy Father which seeth in secret shall reward thee openly.

Mark 6:46

And when he had sent them away, he departed into a mountain to pray.

1 John 5:14-15

And this is the confidence that we have in him, that, if we ask any thing according to his will, he heareth us: [15] And if we know that he hear us, whatsoever we ask, we know that we have the petitions that we desired of him.

Following Jesus' instructions, Peter turned to the body and commanded, "Tabitha, arise." Peter had great faith in Jesus. The Lord wanted Dorcas raised from the dead. Peter responded in compassion to the call delivered by the two men. Peter cleared the room and prayed to the Lord seeking His will. Peter listened to the Lord. He called upon Tabitha to arise, through the power of Jesus. Tabitha arose.

The result of raising Tabitha from the dead is that many believed and it opened the door for evangelism in the area. God gave Peter the vision to carry the gospel to the Gentiles while he was in Joppa. The raising of Tabitha from the dead was a foretaste of the resurrection of all believers to life eternal. Because Tabitha was raised, many turned to the Lord for salvation. They turned from spiritual death to spiritual life.

John 5:24

Verily, verily, I say unto you, He that heareth my word, and believeth on him that sent me, hath everlasting life, and shall not come into condemnation; but is passed from death unto life.

John 3:16

For God so loved the world, that he gave his only begotten Son, that whosoever believeth in him should not perish, but have everlasting life.

The Bible offers these accounts of healing and of raising the dead so that we can know with confidence that the Lord is living and still performing miracles today. He is not walking as a human on earth, but is instead using believers to do His work. The Lord will use any believer who has faith and comes to Him in prayer.

CHAPTER FOUR

THE BELIEVER'S RESPONSIBILITY

Every believer has the responsibility to care and pray for the sick.

James 5:14-16

Is any sick among you? let him call for the elders of the church; and let them pray over him, anointing him with oil in the name of the Lord: [15] And the prayer of faith shall save the sick, and the Lord shall raise him up; and if he have committed sins, they shall be forgiven him. [16] Confess your faults one to another, and pray one for another, that ye may be healed. The effectual fervent prayer of a righteous man availeth much.

Matthew 25:35-36

For I was an hungred, and ye gave me meat: I was thirsty, and ye gave me drink: I was a stranger, and ye took me in: [36] Naked, and ye clothed me: I was sick, and ye visited me: I was in prison, and ye came unto me.

Matthew 25:37-40

Then shall the righteous answer him, saying, Lord, when saw we thee an hungred, and fed thee? or thirsty, and gave thee drink? [38] When saw we thee a stranger, and took thee in? or naked, and clothed thee? [39] Or when saw we thee sick, or in prison, and came unto thee? [40] And the King shall answer and say unto them, Verily I say unto you, Inasmuch as ye have done it unto one of the least of these my brethren, ye have done it unto me.

Matthew 25:44-46

Then shall they also answer him, saying, Lord, when saw we thee an hungred, or athirst, or a stranger, or naked, or sick, or in prison, and did not minister unto thee? [45] Then shall he answer them, saying, Verily I say unto you, Inasmuch as ye did it not to one of the least of these, ye did it not to me. [46] And these shall go away into everlasting punishment: but the righteous into life eternal.

Clearly, the Lord expects believers to minister to the sick. Not only does scripture tell us that we are to minister to them, it tells us that by turning our backs on the sick we are turning our back on Him.

Everlasting punishment is the price to pay for turning one's back on Jesus or the sick. Scripture tells a beautiful story of how we are to love our neighbor and care for the sick.

The Parable of the Good Samaritan

Luke 10:27-37

And he answering said, Thou shalt love the Lord thy God with all thy heart, and with all thy soul, and with all thy strength, and with all thy mind; and thy neighbour as thyself. [28] And he said unto him, Thou hast answered right: this do, and thou shalt live. [29] But he, willing to justify himself, said unto Jesus, And who is my neighbour? [30] And Jesus answering said, A certain man went down from Jerusalem to Jericho, and fell among thieves, which stripped him of his raiment, and wounded him, and departed, leaving him half dead. [31] And by chance there came down a certain priest that way: and when he saw him, he passed by on the other side. [32] And likewise a Levite, when he was at the place, came and looked on him, and passed by on the other side. [33] But a certain Samaritan, as he journeyed, came where he was: and when he saw him, he had compassion on him, [34] And went to him, and bound up his wounds, pouring in oil and wine, and set him on his own beast, and brought him to an inn, and took care of him. [35] And on the morrow when he departed, he took out two pence, and gave them to the host, and said unto him, Take care of him; and whatsoever thou spendest more, when I come again, I will repay thee. [36] Which now of these three, thinkest thou, was neighbour unto him that fell among the thieves? [37] And he said, He that shewed mercy on him. Then said Jesus unto him, Go, and do thou likewise.

The story of the Good Samaritan answers the questions of how we inherit eternal life, who our neighbor is, and what our responsibility is as a believer. Scripture spells out clearly what is required to attain eternal life. When Jesus questioned the lawyer about what he had read in scripture and his understanding, the lawyer responded by quoting Deuteronomy 6:5 and Leviticus 19:18. Remember that at this time they had only the Old Testament. Scripture was carried in a small box called a phylactery. These boxes were worn during prayer. To the lawyer, eternal life was gained by doing works. Jesus responded to the lawyer by telling the story of the Good Samaritan.

Deut. 6:5

And thou shalt love the Lord thy God with all thine heart, and with all thy soul, and with all thy might.

Leviticus 19:18

Thou shalt not avenge, nor bear any grudge against the children of thy people, but thou shalt love thy neighbour as thyself: I am the Lord.

Deut. 6:3

Hear therefore, O Israel, and observe to do it; that it may be well with thee, and that ye may increase mightily, as the Lord God of thy fathers hath promised thee, in the land that floweth with milk and honey.

Deut. 10:12

And now, Israel, what doth the Lord thy God require of thee, but to fear the Lord thy God, to walk in all his ways, and to love him, and to serve the Lord thy God with all thy heart and with all thy soul,

Deut. 11:1

Therefore thou shalt love the Lord thy God, and keep his charge, and his statutes, and his judgments, and his commandments, alway.

Joshua 22:5

But take diligent heed to do the commandment and the law, which Moses the servant of the Lord charged you, to love the Lord your God, and to walk in all his ways, and to keep his commandments, and to cleave unto him, and to serve him with all your heart and with all your soul.

We learn from these scriptures that we are to love God. There must be a demonstration or act to show this love. Love cannot be dormant. We also learn from this story that we are to love our neighbor as ourself. This love is also to be active. Loving our neighbor is an act of showing our love for God. Loving our neighbor proves our love for God. Obedience is also required for eternal life.

Leviticus 19:34

But the stranger that dwelleth with you shall be unto you as one born among you, and thou shalt love him as thyself; for ye were strangers in the land of Egypt: I am the Lord your God.

1 John 3:14

We know that we have passed from death unto life, because we love the brethren. He that loveth not his brother abideth in death.

1 John 4:20-21

If a man say, I love God, and hateth his brother, he is a liar: for he that loveth not his brother whom he hath seen, how can he love God whom he hath not seen? [21] And this commandment have we from him, That he who loveth God love his brother also.

Matthew 5:44

But I say unto you, Love your enemies, bless them that curse you, do good to them that hate you, and pray for them which despitefully use you, and persecute you;

Mark 12:31

And the second is like, namely this, Thou shalt love thy neighbour as thyself. There is none other commandment greater than these.

John 13:34-35

A new commandment I give unto you, That ye love one another; as I have loved you, that ye also love one another. [35] By this shall all men know that ye are my disciples, if ye have love one to another.

John 15:12

This is my commandment, That ye love one another, as I have loved you.

Romans 13:8-10

Owe no man any thing, but to love one another: for he that loveth another hath fulfilled the law. [9] For this, Thou shalt not commit adultery, Thou shalt not kill, Thou shalt not steal, Thou shalt not bear false witness, Thou shalt not covet; and if there be any other commandment, it is briefly comprehended in this saying, namely, Thou shalt love thy neighbour as thyself. [10] Love worketh no ill to his neighbour: therefore love is the fulfilling of the law.

Galatians 5:14

For all the law is fulfilled in one word, even in this; Thou shalt love thy neighbour as thyself.

James 2:8

If ye fulfil the royal law according to the scripture, Thou shalt love thy neighbour as thyself, ye do well:

1 John 4:7-11

Beloved, let us love one another: for love is of God; and every one that loveth is born of God, and knoweth God. [8] He that loveth not knoweth not God; for God is love. [9] In this was manifested the love of God toward us, because that God sent his only begotten Son into the world, that we might live through him. [10] Herein is love, not that we loved God, but that he loved us, and sent his Son to be the propitiation for our sins. [11] Beloved, if God so loved us, we ought also to love one another.

The lawyer had asked of Jesus, "Who is my neighbor?" Jesus answered this question by telling the story of the Good Samaritan. To understand the point Jesus was making, I think it is important to look at who the Samaritans were.

Samaria was the central part of Palestine. Palestine was a small country, reaching only one hundred twenty miles north to south. The country was divided into three sections: Judea was the southern section, Galilee was the northern section, and Samaria was the central section. The Jews and Samaritans bitterly hated each other.

One reason for this hatred was that the Samarians were half-Jews, or a mixed breed, from birth. Around 720 B.C. the Assyrian king had captured the ten tribes and deported them, scattering them throughout Media. Then he transplanted Assyrians into Samaria to repopulate the land. Intermarriage took place infuriating strict Jews who held to a pure race. The Samaritans were mixed in religion as well. Those who had been transplanted brought their heathen gods with them. The religion of the Samaritans was never again pure Judaism.

When the Jews returned from exile they started to rebuild the temple. They refused to allow the Samaritans to help because they had lost their purity. The Samaritans became bitter and built a rival temple on Mount Gerizim. The Samaritans twisted scripture and accepted only the Pentateuch. They twisted history by claiming that

Abraham offered Isaac, Melchizedek met Abraham and Moses built his first altar on Mt. Gerizim.[8]

In the story of the Good Samaritan, the traveler was being foolish and irresponsible. The road between Jericho and Jerusalem was called *the Way of the Blood* because it was extremely dangerous. It was rare for travelers to travel alone on this 30 mile stretch of road.

Proverbs 22:3

A prudent man foreseeth the evil, and hideth himself: but the simple pass on, and are punished.

The first to pass by the man was a priest. He was a religionist who placed his religion above the man lying in the road. He hurried by, neglecting to stop and offer aid.

Matthew 25:41-43

Then shall he say also unto them on the left hand, Depart from me, ye cursed, into everlasting fire, prepared for the devil and his

---

[8] ***Preachers Outline and Sermon Bible.*** Leadership Ministries Worldwide.

angels: [42] For I was an hungred, and ye gave me no meat: I was thirsty, and ye gave me no drink: [43] I was a stranger, and ye took me not in: naked, and ye clothed me not: sick, and in prison, and ye visited me not.

Luke 12:47

And that servant, which knew his lord's will, and prepared not himself, neither did according to his will, shall be beaten with many stripes.

James 4:17

Therefore to him that knoweth to do good, and doeth it not, to him it is sin.

Micah 6:8

He hath shewed thee, O man, what is good; and what doth the Lord require of thee, but to do justly, and to love mercy, and to walk humbly with thy God?

A Levite also passed by the man. He placed his own safety before compassion. The Levite's heart had enough compassion to walk over and look upon the man, but did not help him.

James 2:14-16

What doth it profit, my brethren, though a man say he hath faith, and have not works? can faith save him? [15] If a brother or sister be naked, and destitute of daily food, [16] And one of you say unto them, Depart in peace, be ye warmed and filled; notwithstanding ye give them not those things which are needful to the body; what doth it profit?

1 John 3:17-18

But whoso hath this world's good, and seeth his brother have need, and shutteth up his bowels of compassion from him, how dwelleth the love of God in him? [18] My little children, let us not love in word, neither in tongue; but in deed and in truth.

Proverbs 21:13

Whoso stoppeth his ears at the cry of the poor, he also shall cry himself, but shall not be heard.

Proverbs 24:11-12

If thou forbear to deliver them that are drawn unto death, and those that are ready to be slain; [12] If thou sayest, Behold, we knew it not; doth not he that pondereth the heart consider it? and he that keepeth thy soul, doth not he know it? and shall not he render to every man according to his works?

Ezekiel 34:4-10

The diseased have ye not strengthened, neither have ye healed that which was sick, neither have ye bound up that which was broken, neither have ye brought again that which was driven away, neither have ye sought that which was lost; but with force and with cruelty have ye ruled them. [5] And they were scattered, because there is no shepherd: and they became meat to all the beasts of the field, when they were scattered. [6] My sheep wandered through all the mountains, and upon every high hill: yea, my flock was scattered upon all the face of the earth, and none did search or seek after them.

[7] Therefore, ye shepherds, hear the word of the Lord; [8] As I live, saith the Lord God, surely because my flock became a prey, and

my flock became meat to every beast of the field, because there was no shepherd, neither did my shepherds search for my flock, but the shepherds fed themselves, and fed not my flock; [9] Therefore, O ye shepherds, hear the word of the Lord; [10] Thus saith the Lord God; Behold, I am against the shepherds; and I will require my flock at their hand, and cause them to cease from feeding the flock; neither shall the shepherds feed themselves any more; for I will deliver my flock from their mouth, that they may not be meat for them.

The next to come upon the man was the Samaritan. He showed compassion and has taught us who our neighbor is. He heard the passionate cry for help from the Jew. The Jew and the Samaritan were not from the same race and the two races were known to hate each other. Yet, the Samaritan showed that he saw a man, a human being, not a Jew or enemy. The Samaritan had compassion for the Jew and helped him by giving of his time, money and energy. He showed his love for God by acting in love toward a fellow man. The Samaritan went beyond the immediate need by seeking care for the man and paying for his care until he could return.

The Lord told the lawyer to go and do what the Samaritan had done, love his neighbor. If the lawyer wanted eternal life, he must do as Jesus pointed out, he must show love and mercy to his neighbor.

Matthew 25:35-40

For I was an hungred, and ye gave me meat: I was thirsty, and ye gave me drink: I was a stranger, and ye took me in: [36] Naked, and ye clothed me: I was sick, and ye visited me: I was in prison, and ye came unto me. [37] Then shall the righteous answer him, saying, Lord, when saw we thee an hungred, and fed thee? or thirsty, and gave thee drink? [38] When saw we thee a stranger, and took thee in? or naked, and clothed thee? [39] Or when saw we thee sick, or in prison, and came unto thee? [40] And the King shall answer and say unto them, Verily I say unto you, Inasmuch as ye have done it unto one of the least of these my brethren, ye have done it unto me.

Romans 12:20

Therefore if thine enemy hunger, feed him; if he thirst, give him drink: for in so doing thou shalt heap coals of fire on his head.

Galatians 6:2

Bear ye one another's burdens, and so fulfil the law of Christ.

Exodus 23:4

If thou meet thine enemy's ox or his ass going astray, thou shalt surely bring it back to him again.

Leviticus 25:35

And if thy brother be waxen poor, and fallen in decay with thee; then thou shalt relieve him: yea, though he be a stranger, or a sojourner; that he may live with thee.

Proverbs 25:21-22

If thine enemy be hungry, give him bread to eat; and if he be thirsty, give him water to drink: [22] For thou shalt heap coals of fire upon his head, and the Lord shall reward thee.

Hebrews 13:3

Remember them that are in bonds, as bound with them; and them which suffer adversity, as being yourselves also in the body.

Deut. 10:17-19

For the Lord your God is God of gods, and Lord of lords, a great God, a mighty, and a terrible, which regardeth not persons, nor taketh reward: [18] He doth execute the judgment of the fatherless and widow, and loveth the stranger, in giving him food and raiment. [19] Love ye therefore the stranger: for ye were strangers in the land of Egypt.

Proverbs 24:17

Rejoice not when thine enemy falleth, and let not thine heart be glad when he stumbleth:

Faith In Jesus

All believers have the ability and responsibility to call upon the Lord when another believer…or a stranger is sick or dying. This has been clearly spelled out in scripture. When we take our pleas to the Lord, we must have faith that He will hear our prayers and respond.

Matthew 17:20

And Jesus said unto them, Because of your unbelief: for verily I say unto you, If ye have faith as a grain of mustard seed, ye shall say unto this mountain, Remove hence to yonder place; and it shall remove; and nothing shall be impossible unto you.

Matthew 21:21

Jesus answered and said unto them, Verily I say unto you, If ye have faith, and doubt not, ye shall not only do this which is done to the fig tree, but also if ye shall say unto this mountain, Be thou removed, and be thou cast into the sea; it shall be done.

Mark 11:22-24

And Jesus answering saith unto them, Have faith in God. [23] For verily I say unto you, That whosoever shall say unto this mountain, Be thou removed, and be thou cast into the sea; and shall not doubt in his heart, but shall believe that those things which he saith shall come to pass; he shall have whatsoever he saith. [24] Therefore I say unto you, What things soever ye desire, when ye pray, believe that ye receive them, and ye shall have them.

Luke 8:50

But when Jesus heard it, he answered him, saying, Fear not: believe only, and she shall be made whole.

2 Chron. 20:20

And they rose early in the morning, and went forth into the wilderness of Tekoa: and as they went forth, Jehoshaphat stood and said, Hear me, O Judah, and ye inhabitants of Jerusalem; Believe in the Lord your God, so shall ye be established; believe his prophets, so shall ye prosper.

Faith is required of both the person praying and the sick.

Mark 9:23

Jesus said unto him, If thou canst believe, all things are possible to him that believeth.

Psalm 37:5

Commit thy way unto the Lord; trust also in him; and he shall bring it to pass.

Matthew 10:32

Whosoever therefore shall confess me before men, him will I confess also before my Father which is in heaven.

Prayer…in faith…from a believer will heal.

James 5:16

Confess your faults one to another, and pray one for another, that ye may be healed. The effectual fervent prayer of a righteous man availeth much.

Matthew 7:7-8

Ask, and it shall be given you; seek, and ye shall find; knock, and it shall be opened unto you: [8] For every one that asketh receiveth; and he that seeketh findeth; and to him that knocketh it shall be opened.

John 16:24

Hitherto have ye asked nothing in my name: ask, and ye shall receive, that your joy may be full.

James 5:13

Is any among you afflicted? let him pray. Is any merry? let him sing psalms.

Prayer from the church elders will heal.

James 5:14-15

Is any sick among you? let him call for the elders of the church; and let them pray over him, anointing him with oil in the name of the Lord: [15] And the prayer of faith shall save the sick, and the Lord shall raise him up; and if he have committed sins, they shall be forgiven him.

The sick referred to in this passage are those who are suffering and shut in, unable to get out and go to the church. In this case, the elders, or leaders of the church are to go to the shut-in. This sick person will be concerned for his health and have faith that the church leaders will earnestly and fervently pray for him. The sick person must believe that he will be healed by the prayer. The church leaders must also have faith that the prayers will bring healing. Faith is the essential ingredient. The prayer and anointing with oil is to be done in the name of the Lord. The elders and the sick must have faith that the Lord alone can heal and that the prayer in His name will bring about healing. They must pray in faith, knowing and expecting God to heal the sick.

Anoint the sick with oil.

James 5:14-15

Is any sick among you? let him call for the elders of the church; and let them pray over him, anointing him with oil in the name of the Lord: [15] And the prayer of faith shall save the sick, and the Lord shall raise him up; and if he have committed sins, they shall be forgiven him.

Oil is a symbol of the Holy Spirit. It is a symbol of the Spirit's presence. The oil helps the sick person to focus and concentrate upon the presence of the Holy Spirit and His power. The sick often have a hard time focusing and concentrating. When one is in great pain it is especially difficult for one to focus. The oil placed on the body helps the sick focus and concentrate on God's power and presence. Oil is also a symbol of God's care comfort, joy and His mercy on us. Oil actually focuses the attention and stirs the sick person to believe in God's mercy. By focusing the attention the sick person's heart can be filled with hope and gladness.

Psalm 45:7

Thou lovest righteousness, and hatest wickedness: therefore God, thy God, hath anointed thee with the oil of gladness above thy fellows.

Hebrews 1:9

Thou hast loved righteousness, and hated iniquity; therefore God, even thy God, hath anointed thee with the oil of gladness above thy fellows.

Matthew 21:22

And all things, whatsoever ye shall ask in prayer, believing, ye shall receive.

Mark 9:23

Jesus said unto him, If thou canst believe, all things are possible to him that believeth.

John 15:7

If ye abide in me, and my words abide in you, ye shall ask what ye will, and it shall be done unto you.

CHAPTER FIVE

EMERGENCY CALLS

It's 2:30 A.M. and the phone rings. An anxious voice on the other end of the phone says that there has been a wreck and one of your church members is in the emergency room. What do you do? Or, It's 2:30 P.M. and you get a call from a sobbing woman who says her husband has just been diagnosed with cancer. What do you do? Maybe you get the word through the prayer chain or you hear just before worship service on Sunday. You may get the word in many different ways. The key is in how you react and how rapidly you respond.

The ministry of comfort is clearly in the hands of the church. Whether you are a pastor or a member of the congregation, you have a call from God to offer comfort to those in trouble. When illness or tragedy hits, a church must be prepared. Many churches have prayer chains or another means of getting the word out when someone needs prayer. It is sad when a person is admitted into the hospital on Wednesday and the pastor doesn't hear about it until Sunday morning. It can be quite embarrassing to the pastor. A little planning ahead of time can prevent this.

Prayer chains are an excellent way to pass the word about prayer needs among the prayer warriors in the church. There should also be in place a system to contact each member in an emergency or in the case of hospitalization or serious illness. In small churches the tree system works well. In this method, each family will receive a call and in turn will call others that have been assigned to them. In larger churches this is a bit more complicated. Some churches have a deacon ministry and part of their service is to call their families when a need or emergency arises.

Whenever possible a pastor should develop a relationship with every member of the flock. In large churches this isn't always possible. People generally feel more comfortable having their pastor called if they know him personally and know that he cares about them. Pastors should be accessible to the flock. I also recommend that pastors make known to the flock that they are available 24/7 in emergencies. A person is more likely to call if they know the pastor has given them permission. But, make sure they understand that it shouldn't be abused. Tell them that like calling 911, it is for emergencies and when abused it takes away from others. Explain to them that you want to know if an accident has happened, or if there is a serious illness. Make sure they know you care. Local hospitals will gladly place a call to a pastor if needed. Some larger churches have on staff a Pastoral Care Pastor who handles this ministry. The members need to know who to call in an emergency.

It is 2:30 A.M. and the phone rings. A member has been involved in a car wreck You are the pastor, or pastoral care person for the church. Get as much information as you can from the person calling. Make sure to get the name of the person in crisis, the name of the hospital, what has happened, and the status of the patient. Also, find out all who were involved and if the family has been reached. It's a good idea to keep a pad of paper and pencil by the phone. Write everything down. It's easy to forget when you've been awakened from a sound sleep. Lift a prayer for the person or persons involved. Then make a determination of what your course of action will be.

Upon arriving at the hospital, identify yourself to the staff. Generally, the hospital staff will allow clergy privileges in entering

ER and other areas. An initial assessment of the situation should be made. Is the patient critical? Is the patient in need of spiritual support from you? Often, the presence of the pastor is enough to comfort the patient. The presence of the pastor is often viewed as the presence of the Lord incarnate. That may sound lofty, but a pastor who truly cares for the flock that the Lord has entrusted to him, is a true blessing. The pastor or pastoral care person should not interfere with patient treatment. If procedures are being performed it is important to not get in the way. The pastor should be in constant prayer. When things have calmed down, the pastor can approach the patient. If the patient is unconscious, a touch by the pastor's hand and a softly spoken prayer is in order. If the patient is conscious, the pastor should make a short visit. He should inquire of the patient how he/she is feeling, and what their concerns are. The pastor is there to provide spiritual support. He should make sure the patient knows that he is there and that if there is anything a patient wants to tell them it is up to them. This must be done in a way as to not frighten the patient and make them think they are dying. Many times a pastor is asked to call someone or to pass on a message. There are times when the patient may want you to hear their prayers or pray with or for them. Let the patient guide the visit, but keep it brief. Always offer to pray with the patient and ask them if there is anything they would like for you to ask in prayer.

The pastor should spend some time with the family and friends who come to the hospital. He should offer to pray with them and allow them time to voice prayers if they want to. Most hospitals have a chapel where you can meet for prayer, or if they are comfortable in the waiting area that is fine too. The important thing is to be available. It's a good idea to have a Bible. Small Bibles are available that can be carried in a pocket or purse. Many times the family finds comfort in listening to a Psalm or some comforting passages. However, the pastor must not make this a time to deliver a sermon. There will be times when the only thing a pastor will do will be to stand ready or to offer a hug. The pastor should assess each situation and follow what God leads him to do.

Patients who come to the emergency room are generally crisis patients. They come to the emergency room for something that can be fixed. Many pastors find it difficult to minister to the patient in crisis. They may find it outside their comfort zone. Ministry in the emergency room lacks privacy and is prone to interruption. The important thing is visibility. The church member who sees his/her pastor in the hospital will find comfort from knowing that the pastor cares enough to be there.

There are some pitfalls that must be avoided. A pastor must never use the time to discuss his own illnesses and situations. The most that should be said is I've been in the hospital and I know it can be frightening. Do not go into details about your surgeries, your broken bones, or your illnesses. The patient needs comfort and care, not your life history. Some pastors are uncomfortable in hospitals. It would be better for him to not go than to go and talk only about himself. Pastors must also avoid the pitfall of being there too long. Each situation is different and should be handled differently. In the case of the emergency room visit, it is imperative that the pastor not prevent the care of the patient. He should stand back and let the medical team do their work. When the time is right, he should move toward the patient and stay just long enough to pray and inquire of the patient. More time can be spent with the family. If there is no family present and the patient asks you to stay with them, then by all means do so. Assess each situation. Another pitfall to avoid is that of spreading the word when the patient does not want it. There are times when the patient for whatever reason, does not want others to know what is happening. Perhaps the patient had a car wreck and feels guilty and does not want others to know. It is not wise for the pastor to call on church members to fill the waiting room to pray for the patient, if the patient desires privacy.

If the patient is treated and discharged, the pastor should follow up with a telephone call or visit. The person should be assured that he/she did the right thing in notifying you because you care. The follow up re-enforces the fact that you care. You may not have the time or feel it is necessary to visit, but the minimum of a phone call is in order. If that person has extensive injuries, contact should be made regularly.

If the patient is admitted, then follow up care at the hospital is in order. In these days of HMO's most people have relatively short hospital stays. It's a good idea to call ahead to make sure the patient is still hospitalized and that the patient is up to a visit. This will also give you the opportunity to speak to the patient or a family member to determine any needs. If the patient is going to be in the hospital for an extended amount of time, ask about any surgeries or procedures that they will want specific prayer for and ask them if they want you present. Many times a patient will want their pastor to pray with them before surgery. At other times the patient may feel that having the pastor present is really not necessary. In large churches, sometimes it is impossible for a pastor to do this. In those cases, a pastoral care person should be available and the members should be made aware that this person is providing pastoral care for the pastor. There have been many hurt feelings because the pastor was at the hospital for one person's surgery but missed someone else's surgery. Many churches now have home groups that provide care for one another. In cases like that, the visits may be made by a member of the hospitalized person's home group.

When faced with sudden illness or injury, people will generally move closer to or away from God. This time can be a wake up call to the person to get things right with the Lord. It will often cause the person to repent from behavior that they know is against God's will.

An illness or serious injury can be used by the Lord to bring a lost sheep back into the flock. There are some who blame God for their troubles. The pastor who is wise will be prepared to handle both reactions.

SCRIPTURE THAT CAN BE USED TO COMFORT

Realize that God is with you.

Psalm 34:18

The LORD *is* nigh unto them that are of a broken heart; and saveth such as be of a contrite spirit. (God is close)

Job 13:27

Thou puttest my feet also in the stocks, and lookest narrowly unto all my paths; thou settest a print upon the heels of my feet. (God is aware of what you are going through)

Nahum 1:7

The LORD *is* good, a strong hold in the day of trouble; and he knoweth them that trust in him. (God cares and is a refuge in times of trouble)

Hebrews 4:16

Let us therefore come boldly unto the throne of grace, that we may obtain mercy, and find grace to help in time of need. (God wants to help us)

Release the hurt.

Psalm 10:14

Thou hast seen *it;* for thou beholdest mischief and spite, to requite *it* with thy hand: the poor committeth himself unto thee; thou art the helper of the fatherless. (Release the hurt to God)

Rely on God's Resources

Psalm 119:25

My soul cleaveth unto the dust: quicken thou me according to thy word. (Read God's Word…the Bible)

Romans 15:13

Now the God of hope fill you with all joy and peace in believing, that ye may abound in hope, through the power of the Holy Ghost. (God's Spirit brings comfort)

2 Cor. 1:3-4

Blessed *be* God, even the Father of our Lord Jesus Christ, the Father of mercies, and the God of all comfort; 4Who comforteth us in all our tribulation, that we may be able to comfort them which are in any trouble, by the comfort wherewith we ourselves are comforted of God. (Rely on others Christians)

CHAPTER SIX

CARE OF THE CHRONICALLY ILL

Care of the Chronically Ill

Chronically ill patients are patients who have an illness that has no cure and requires treatment over a period of time. Chronically ill patients come to the hospital for something that can't be fixed, but needs to be followed and treated. Those with chronic illnesses will sometimes have a crisis situation, which will require them to seek immediate help. Pastors who know their flock, know of those in the flock who have chronic illnesses. The pastor should keep them in his prayers. He should ask the member and family to keep him informed of any changes in the person's health. Many times there will be an acute episode that requires hospitalization, bed rest, or some other form of care. If the pastor is advised when an acute situation arises, he can minister to the member accordingly. There are many illnesses and diseases, which are chronic. Heart Disease, MS, HIV, and many, many other diseases can be chronic and debilitating. Chronic diseases may continue indefinitely and ultimately result in death or they may continue for the remainder of the person's life but not be life threatening.

Guideline for hospital visits

Matthew 25:36

Naked, and ye clothed me: I was sick, and ye visited me: I was in prison, and ye came unto me.

Call ahead to confirm that the patient is still in the hospital if you plan to visit a patient in the hospital. Ask to be connected to the patient's room. Talk to the patient and ask if they feel up to a visit. Be sensitive to what they say. The patient may feel exhausted but fear hurting the pastor's feeling by saying they aren't up to a visit. Ask if there are any tests or therapies scheduled and when would be a good time for a visit. Always tell the patient that if they are not up to a visit that you would be happy to come at a time when they are feeling better. The pastor should allow the patient to set the time whenever possible.

Stop at the nurse's station when you arrive on the patient's floor. Identify yourself and ask to speak to the patient's nurse. The pastor should ask the nurse if there is anything that he should know.

Sometimes the nurse will give you some insight into the patient's day. They may tell you that the patient has had some bad news or that the therapy session was particularly difficult. It is also a good idea to ask the nurse about any precautions you should take. The pastor should wash his hands before entering a patient's room so that he does not carry germs in that will expose the patient. **NEVER** visit a patient if you have a communicable disease. This means a cold or anything that can be passed on to the patient.

Let common sense be your guide in the length of visit. If the patient has just undergone surgery and is weak, a short visit is in line. A patient who has been in-patient for a length of time may like a longer visit. Have an amount of time on your mind but always take your cue from the patient.

The pastor should gather information during his visit. Allow the patient time to tell you about his/her illness. Many times the family will want to do this, but it is important to let the patient talk if he /she wants to. Allowing the patient to speak will also let everyone know that the patient understands what is happening. It will also send up a red flag if there are misunderstandings between the patient and family. The patient may be frightened and allowing them to talk will help ease that fear. The pastor should listen to the patient and family for clues as to how the church can minister to them. Assessing the patient's spiritual condition is covered in a later chapter.

In chronically ill patients I have found that asking some leading questions will open the lines of communication about how the person is really feeling. I quite often ask the patient how the disease has affected his/her life. By asking this question I am opening the door for the patient to talk about things like unfulfilled dreams, problems with family or work, or anything at all that may be on their mind. I also ask what the hardest thing has been for them to deal with. When I ask this question to a patient in the hospital it is almost always answered that they miss being at home. A person struggling with cancer who is hospitalized frequently will often say they don't like being away from home. I have seldom heard anyone respond that pain has been the hardest thing to deal with. Most patients handle the physical aspects of the disease better than the emotional aspects.

The visit should include three forms of communication. There should be talking, listening and touching. The patient should be given the opportunity to talk. Sometimes simply talking about problems will help. The pastor doesn't have to have all the answers. The patient may ask questions or may just want to talk to someone he/she trusts. It is important for the pastor to listen. The pastor must show understanding and acceptance. He should not back away or act shocked at what the patient says. Touching the patient is also important. Unless strict instructions have been given to not touch the patient, the pastor should make physical contact. A gentle touch on the hand can relay the message that you care. The patient whose hand the pastor holds will feel reassured and cared for. The gift of touch can be the most valued of all gifts to a patient.

In concluding the visit, the pastor should ask the patient if he would like prayer. Many people don't like to pray out loud in front of others, especially their pastor, so clearly ask, "would you like for me to pray for you?" I also ask what in particular the patient would like for me to pray. This gives the patient a chance to be open about what is on his/her heart. The patient may have concerns about other family members, about test results, or about anything at all. The pastor must be attentive and listen carefully. If you need to take notes, then take them. Don't ask a patient what they need prayer for then forget them in prayer. The pastor can also conclude the visit by offering to read scripture. The patient may have a favorite passage or a Psalm that has special meaning. I have covered in a separate section some passages that offer comfort to the patient.

Sometimes when the pastor enters the hospital room there are others present. This can present a challenge to the pastor. He may sense that the patient would like some time alone with him. This can be handled by offering to sit with the patient and allow the others to take a break or go for some coffee. The pastor can also tell the patient that he will return later and allow him/her time to visit with the others first. Each situation has to be handled by the cue of the patient. If the family wants time away from the patient to talk to the pastor, he may suggest going for coffee or requesting from the staff an area where they can talk in private. There is usually a conference room available for family use. This time can be critical to the family. Pastors can open many doors by being attentive to the needs of the family and patient.

The patient's pastor plays a key role in the treatment of the patient. It is during the time of illness that many begin to question their spirituality. Each case is different. Each patient is different. When my son was fighting cancer, pastoral visits were very uplifting to my family. Our pastor is a very loving, compassionate man. His presence brought comfort and the feeling that he was there as the Lord incarnate. Just as Jesus cared for the sick, so should the pastor.

Home Visits

Generally, it is more comfortable for a pastor to visit the sick in their home. The setting is private and comfortable. When the pastor arrives at the home, he should make those in the home comfortable with his presence. He can do this by offering a hug and sitting down to talk with the family. This is a time when the pastor needs to show his love and concern. The pastor needs to tune in to the feelings of the family. Many times the spouse of the sick person will have concerns that they would like to share. As stated previously, during illness and crisis situations, people will either move closer to God or will turn away. The pastor who is sensitive to the feelings and who listens carefully will be able to tell which direction the family member or sick is going.

The pastor needs to be observant to assess the situation. He should look around the room for signs that could give him an insight into the patient's life. If there are many cards and flowers, the person probably has a good support system in place with many friends and family that care about him. If the home is without cards, flowers, or anything that might indicate outside support, then he may be dealing with a person who is alone or lonely. The pastor should also observe the way family members treat the sick person. This can reveal a lot about family dynamics. Doing these things is not meant to be nosy, but to give insight in to the best approach to ministry to the sick. It will give the pastor the sense of how the family is coping with the illness and what support the sick person has. The pastor will become more comfortable in doing this and will become better at reading the signs the more he does it.

As in a hospital visit, the home visit should include talking, listening and touching. A patient may feel more at ease talking in the privacy of their own home. Getting the patient to talk will help ease anxiety and depression. Simple direct questions will bring good results. I have often just asked the patient what they would like to talk about, or if they have anything on their mind that they would like to have me listen to. These questions are simple and direct. This provides an opening yet isn't pushy. The pastor who routinely visits a chronically or terminally ill person will become more comfortable in doing this.

For some it can be difficult to approach spiritual matters. Again, simple, direct questions are a good approach. The questions should not embarrass the patient or make them uncomfortable. The pastor may ask how the patient feels about God during the illness. This question is direct and leaves the door open for discussion. It's a question that you can draw on to engage the patient in conversation. Reflective questions work well because they cause the patient to reflect on how they are feeling. It is very important to allow the patient time to answer the questions. Sometimes the patient will hesitate, but be patient and allow time. Often it is hard to find a way to express oneself. By rushing an answer the person may get the impression that you are in a hurry.

The art of listening involves the whole body. Whether in a hospital or at home, the pastor should sit when talking to the patient. This communicates to the person that you intend to spend time and that you are interested in listening. The pastor or pastoral care person should look relaxed and comfortable. I have made hospital visits with other pastoral care providers who were very uneasy with the role and it showed in their actions. It is also important to maintain eye contact while the patient is talking. There will be times when the patient may become emotional or embarrassed. The important thing is to maintain contact. If it is an awkward time for the patient, take the patient's hand and remain close. Never back away because you feel awkward.

Most communication is nonverbal. The body must show that you are listening. The listener should tilt the head and nod from time to time. The lips should be in a relaxed position and the listener should smile when appropriate. Leaning forward can signal concern and caring. The posture should remain open with the arms resting comfortably at the side or on the lap. The pastor may want to hold the person's hand.

When one is listening properly one is thinking about what the person is saying, not rehearsing in the mind the response. The patient should be allowed to speak without interruption. If there is a pause, allow time for the patient to collect thoughts and continue. The listener does not have to agree with what the patient is saying. The patient may just need someone to listen as he/she sounds off. The listener may at times feel uncomfortable but should not change the subject.

It can be helpful to encourage the patient to reminisce. This can be an enjoyable time, especially for the older patient. This may give them a chance to reflect on their life and find meaning in it. As they look back on past experiences it reminds them how they got through the tough times and how things got better.

The objective of sensitive listening is to understand as completely as possible the patient's feelings. The better the communication the better you will understand the patient's feelings. The more you work at understanding the patient's feelings, the more support you are giving.[9]

Touching the patient is one of the most important ways to communicate with the patient. The need to be touched is innate in human beings. Contact causes the patient to feel more comfortable and peaceful. Depriving one of touch can lead to despondency, loss of appetite, apathy, and a decline in efficient functioning.[10] A person who is ill needs more physical contact than a healthy one.

When ministering to a family with a newly diagnosed family member, the pastor may encounter many spiritual questions. Often someone will ask, "Why Tom?" They may even interpret illness as an act of God for punishment for something in the patient's life. Some

---

[9] Anderson, Monnie. Ideas for Hospital Ministries. New Hope, Birmingham, AL, 1992.
[10] Ibid. p.11

diseases are a direct result of a person's lifestyle, such as a smoker who develops lung cancer or a homosexual who gets AIDS. But God does not cause the person to get sick. Illness happens and no one is exempt from getting ill. Even the person who eats right and gets plenty of exercise may still get a disease. Many things factor into our health. The point is that the pastor will encounter questions when ministering to the sick so he better study and be prepared to answer the questions.

It is a good idea to have something set up ahead of time in the church for pastoral visits. It can tremendously life the spirits of the sick or chronically ill to be paid a visit by the pastor. It can also be a blessing to the pastor. Pastoral Care within the church is an area that requires dedication and commitment. Many churches have a team of gifted people in place to make visits in the home when a member is sick. Often, Sunday school teachers will visit those in their class when sick. For home visits, all members can minister to those in need. All have gifts that can be used in this ministry. A person gifted in music can sing a song, or one gifted in helps could pitch in and help around the house. The system should be in place before needed. It can be very hurtful to a member if it appears that no one in the church, especially the pastor, cares.

Care of the chronically ill takes time and effort. Pastors who tend to pastoral care by themselves should set aside enough time through the week to minister in the home and hospital. They must also be prepared in crisis situations to drop everything and go where needed. In this day of technology, it is easy to stay in touch. A pager or cell phone is a good way to accomplish that. Business cards could be given to all members, which would include the pastor's phone number and pager number.

A chronically ill patient who is regularly visited by the pastor has the opportunity to build a solid relationship. The pastor becomes close to the patient allowing that patient to openly talk about anything. This can be very important to a terminally ill patient. Many times the patient will have life experiences that they will want to tell the pastor. There may be some things that have happened in the past that they need to talk about. The time given to a terminally ill patient allows them to mend fences, to see things in a new light, and to draw closer to God. The pastor who counsels the terminally ill is truly blessed.

Guided Imagery

In ministering to the critically ill, the terminally ill, and those near death, guided imagery can be an effective way to calm and relax the patient. In my ministry I have used this technique successfully when a patient was in despair.

Begin by playing some soft background music. I like to use a tape with sounds of the ocean. Pick up the rhythm of the tape in both your speech and your breathing. Slowly and softly begin talking with the tape. Lead the patient into a relaxing scene. It may go something like the following:

"Close your eyes and walk with me on the beach. (Speak ever so softly and slowly.) The waves are breaking and white foam washes ashore. You are walking close to the water. Another wave is coming in and you allow your toes to touch the water. It feels warm. More waves are coming. You wade in to your knees. You are a child again.

You hear sea gulls flying overhead. One lands on the beach. Imagine that the sea gull was sent to take away all your cares and worries. Place all those cares and worries on the wings of the sea gull. As the sea gull begins to fly away you realize that it was Jesus who took away all that burdened your heart. The sun is shining brighter now. You feel much more relaxed and lighter. Continue walking and listening to the sounds. Smell the ocean breeze. When you feel calm and relaxed open your eyes."

Tapes with nature sounds can also be very relaxing. They are available in many stores and are a good investment. Choose you story to go with the person and their illness. I have also used the poem "Footprints in the Sand" as guided imagery with a patient. I always carry a copy of the poem with me and have given it to many patients. The image of being carried by the Lord in times of illness, or in trials is very comforting. I have played background ocean sounds while reading the poem. Then I have instructed the patient to feel Jesus' arms around them. It is very comforting to the patient. I tell them that Jesus is always with them and that He loves them.

The use of guided imagery and tapes to calm and relax is a useful tool. If the pastor is uncomfortable with doing it then he should follow his own heart. I have found in working with terminally ill patients especially, that guided imagery works well for me.

Surgical Visits

All churches should have a plan in place to deal with medical emergencies and surgeries. Planned surgeries are easier to handle than emergencies, because you usually have ample time to include it in your schedule. It is not wise for the pastor to only go to the hospital for some surgeries and patients and not others. All of God's children are important to Him and should be to us. Little Tommy's surgery is just as important to attend as is John's by-pass. The church may have others assigned to surgical visits. Deacons and deacon wives should know their families and could offer their support and God's comfort during this time.

It is good to offer to pray with the patient before surgery. I have found that praying for God's blessing on the surgeon and guidance for his hands, along with easing the anxiety and healing are comforting to the patient. The pastor who knows the patient will be able to offer personal prayers, mentioning family members by name. The pastor who does this must be careful not to exclude anyone. The prayers must come from a sincere heart. This isn't a time to impress others with wordy prayers filled with words like thee and thou. A heartfelt prayer will give the patient a sense of comfort and uplifting faith.

It can be a great comfort to have someone sit with you while a loved one is going through surgery. Often family members will put up a brave front for the sick but when they've been taken to surgery their emotions begin to surface. The pastoral care provider needs to be alert and offer comfort and support. Many times a reassuring hug or just being there will be all that is needed to give the family strength. Words are not always necessary. I have found that by observing and using my intuition, I can determine what the family needs from me. It's always appropriate to offer prayer or offer to read scripture. If the family so desires, you can move to a secluded area or to the chapel. A prayer ended with the Lord's Prayer gives others the opportunity to participate if they so desire. This can also be a time to engage the family in sharing their feelings. Some families do not openly show emotions while others openly express feelings and emotions. Some people will open up to the pastoral care provider in a private conversation. This is a time to just be there and be available. You may be engaged in an outpouring of emotions, or you may get coffee for those waiting. The role is not clear-cut; each situation and instance is different.

POST OP

When the surgery is complete the patient will be moved to post op recovery. During this time the patient's vital signs are monitored while they come out of anesthesia. Generally this is when the surgeon speaks to the family. If the family wishes, the pastor may accompany them to hear the results of the surgery. It can be a time of relief and thanksgiving or a time of despair and anxiety.

The pastor, deacon, or pastoral care giver must be prepared to listen carefully to all that is said in a physician consultation. Family members are often confused and unable to grasp all that is being said. Bad news is never easy to accept. Listen carefully and get the facts. Write them down if possible. Many times it will be the pastor who will have the facts when the family begins to question what was said. The pastor or pastoral care provider should seek God's guidance and the help of the Holy Spirit as he/she ministers to the family and patient. The pastor must be sensitive and compassionate.

After the consultation with the doctor, there may be others waiting to hear what the doctor said. Be on hand to help in relaying this information. However, do not take it upon yourself to start spreading the word. Inquire from the nearest family member what if anything they would like for you to do. You may be called on to stand by in case someone reacts to the news in a strong way. It is best to stay in the background and take the lead from the family. They may want you to call others or they may want to do it themselves. Do not presume to know what is wanted, ask first and be prepared to do what the family wishes.

The consultation may produce "good news" as well as bad. Many times the findings of surgery puts to rest fears that the patient may have a dreaded illness. This is a time of thanksgiving. Sensitivity to others must be realized. The surgical waiting room is not the place to deliver the news. There is often an adjoining family room or chapel for this purpose. It is good to pass along "bad news" as well as "good news" in private. This is done to ensure privacy and sensitivity toward others.

When the patient has come out of anesthesia, he/she is either discharged or admitted. The discharged patient should be followed up by a home visit or a phone call. Churches should have a system in place to handle the needs of those who are sick. A patient who has been admitted should be visited while in the hospital. The pastor should stay informed of the patient's condition. The pastor should also stay available to the family. In large churches the pastor may not have time in his busy schedule to do a thorough follow up. In those churches it is advisable that deacons or someone assigned to pastoral care fill in for the pastor.

If the surgical patent becomes a chronic care patient, the spiritual care provider should follow those steps in the section on chronically ill patients. Many patients will have spiritual questions following a major surgery. The wise pastor will be prepared for this ahead of time.

Scripture for the Sick

Romans 8:16-25

The Spirit itself beareth witness with our spirit, that we are the children of God: 17And if children, then heirs; heirs of God, and joint-heirs with Christ; if so be that we suffer with *him,* that we may be also glorified together.

Romans 8:38-39

For I am persuaded, that neither death, nor life, nor angels, nor principalities, nor powers, nor things present, nor things to come, 39Nor height, nor depth, nor any other creature, shall be able to separate us from the love of God, which is in Christ Jesus our Lord.

Hebrews 6:11

And we desire that every one of you do shew the same diligence to the full assurance of hope unto the end:

Hebrews 6:19

Which *hope* we have as an anchor of the soul, both sure and stedfast, and which entereth into that within the veil;

Psalm 55:22

Cast thy burden upon the LORD, and he shall sustain thee: he shall never suffer the righteous to be moved.

Ephes. 3:20

Now unto him that is able to do exceeding abundantly above all that we ask or think, according to the power that worketh in us,

Psalm 138:3

In the day when I cried thou answeredst me, *and* strengthenedst me *with* strength in my soul.

Psalm 118:8

It is better to trust in the LORD than to put confidence in man.

Proverbs 3:5

Trust in the LORD with all thine heart; and lean not unto thine own understanding.

Matthew 15:28

Then Jesus answered and said unto her, O woman, great *is* thy faith: be it unto thee even as thou wilt. And her daughter was made whole from that very hour.

Deut. 7:9

Know therefore that the LORD thy God, he *is* God, the faithful God, which keepeth covenant and mercy with them that love him and keep his commandments to a thousand generations;

Psalm 106:1

Praise ye the LORD. O give thanks unto the LORD; for *he is* good: for his mercy *endureth* for ever.

Jude 1:21

Keep yourselves in the love of God, looking for the mercy of our Lord Jesus Christ unto eternal life.

CHAPTER SEVEN

MINISTRY TO THE TERMINALLY ILL

Terminally ill patients are those who have a disease or illness that cannot be cured and the patients are near the end of life. Sometimes the person is diagnosed with cancer that has no treatment and the person is told almost immediately that they are terminal. For others, they may have a disease that is treatable but has no cure. A person with a chronic illness such as AIDS or Leukemia may have periods where he/she gets better then worse which are called "peaks and valleys." Some diseases are progressive and the patient may get worse and lose functions during their disease. A person with cancer may suffer over a long period of time before death. A patient who was injured in a car wreck may survive for a short time but then die.

Ministry to the terminally ill patient can be a real blessing. The time spent in ministry to a person who is coming close to the end of life can also be very emotionally draining to the pastor. It is during this time that many decisions about care have to be made and often the family needs someone to talk to. It is important for the pastor to know a bit about care of a terminally ill person so that he can understand the decisions that are put before them. It isn't the responsibility of the pastor to make the decisions but it is helpful if he is familiar with procedures and terminology. I will discuss in this section some of those decisions that face the terminally ill patient and the family.

A person's death is unique. Ministry to the dying person should not fit a mold, but rather should fit the person and their needs. People who are dying need intimate, natural, honest relationships. In ministry to the dying, one should bring both strengths and vulnerabilities to the bedside. It is OK to cry. Empathize with the patient and give them your undivided attention. When listening, do not judge. Pay close attention to feelings and non-verbal clues. The patient may be discovering truths about themselves and may want to share what they are learning. Allow the patient as much time as they need to talk. The pastor may comfort the frightened patient by holding the hand and listening to stories. He may engage the patient in reflecting by asking the patient about his/her childhood or other lifetime experiences. The simple presence of the pastor has a healing power in itself. As the patient nears death he/she may go to higher dimension of spiritual awareness. Near death, the attention wanders from the exterior and turns inward. The dying often ask themselves questions about the life they have lived. Christians can draw on their faith in God's promises for comfort. Pastors help patients and family members identify their values regarding end-of-life treatment choices. By talking to the patient and family about their values and beliefs in this are you can help them reduce expensive, unwanted care.[11]

Phases of a life-threatening illness

A life threatening illness may be described as having four phases, including the phase before diagnosis, the acute phase, the chronic phase, and recovery or death. The first phase is a time when a person realizes that he/she may be sick. This time would include the time of initial doctor visits when testing is done and ends when the person is told the diagnosis. The acute phase occurs when the diagnosis is made and decisions are made as to the treatment. The chronic phase is the period between diagnosis and the result of treatment. During this time the person tries to cope with life while undergoing treatment and dealing with side effects. During the recovery phase, people cope with the social, mental, physical, religious, and financial aspects of their

[11] Daly, G. (2000). Ethics and Economics. *Nursing Economics.*

illness. The terminal phase occurs when death is likely. The focus then changes from cure to providing comfort and pain relief. The patient often focuses on spiritual matters at this time. [12]

Five Stages in the Process of Coming to Terms with Dying

There are five stages in the process of coming to terms with dying: denial, anger, bargaining, depression, and acceptance. Not all those at the end of life will go through each stage, and they may come in a different order. They may feel angry since no one seems to understand what they are going through or their needs. The pastor should reassure the dying person that it is normal to feel frustration and anger. Dying brings out many suppressed emotions. By being patient with the person and allowing them to work through their emotions they will be more easily able to return to calmness and serenity. The pastor doesn't have to always have wise words to say. The important thing is to be present, to allow the patient to talk, to listen attentively, and to allow the patient to express his/her emotions.

---

[12] University of Pennsylvania Cancer Center, NCI/PDQ Patient Information:Grief, Loss, and Bereavement. June 2000.

The pastor must not be judgmental. The pastor must be accepting and allow the patient to speak freely. Sometimes when a person is near death, a need to talk about sins of the past will arise. If the person is lost, this may be the last opportunity to hear the gospel. The pastor should be prepared to share the gospel and lead the person to Christ.[13]

Signs of Impending Death

Bill Moyers in his program *"On Our Own Terms,"* described how to prepare for the death of a Loved one. The following section on the signs of impending death comes from that program. The information for that program came from an article titled "Preparing for the Death of a Loved One."[14] There are physical, emotional, spiritual and mental signs that death is impending. There are natural changes that happen during the dying process as the body prepares to die. Not all patients will have all signs and they will not all follow the same order. I spent the last couple of months with my grandmother as she prepared to die and have personally seen many of these signs and symptoms. The

---

[13] Rinpoche, Sogyal. "Showing Unconditional Love," The Tibetan Book of Living and Dying. Harper, San Francisco.

[14] Metropolitan Hospice of Greater New York, *Preparing for the Death of a Loved One.*

time spent with her was one of the greatest learning experiences in my ministry. It was more importantly the time when I was closest to my grandmother.

I feel it is important for the pastoral caregiver to understand and recognize the signs of impending death. It will make it less of a shock to know what to expect when entering the room of a person near death. It also helps the pastor know how to better minister to the patient and family.

Fluid and Food Decrease

The patient usually has little interest in eating and drinking. The person should be allowed to eat and drink whatever is appetizing to them, but any nourishment should be taken slowly and in small amounts. Let the person decide how much and when to eat and drink and do not force it on them. Be careful of decreases in swallowing ability, and do not force fluids if the person coughs soon after. Reflexes needed to swallow may be slugish. Forcing fluids and food could cause choking. Small chips of ice, frozen juices, or Popsicles may be refreshing in the mouth.

The person's body lets him/her know when it no longer desires or can tolerate foods or liquids. The loss of this desire is a signal that the person is preparing to die. It is not a painful process. Dehydration does not make them uncomfortable. For my grandmother, we used glycerine swabs to moisten her mouth and vaseline on her lips to keep them moist.

Decreased Socialization

As the person approaches death, he/she will begin to close in the circle of visitors. You may find that the person gives up things that were once important. There will be times when the patient is weak and tired and will not want visitors.

With my grandmother, in her last couple of weeks she began asking that only immediate family visit for short periods of time. The closer she got to the end it narrowed to only those of us involved in her care. Her pastor continued to make brief visits, which lifted her spirits. The presence of a pastor is a connection to God. When the pastor is present the patient may feel a holy presence. It has been described by some as the Lord incarnate.

Sleeping

The nearer the person comes to the end, the more time the person will sleep and be unresponsive. As I said earlier, not all people have all signs or in the same order. But, as a person's metabolism slows they will sleep more and become harder to arouse. At this point, the pastor may hold the person's hand and speak softly. He may choose this time to pray, or read scripture to the person. Hearing is the last of the senses to go, so don't assume that the person can't hear. Be careful not to say anything upsetting that you would not want the patient to hear. Use this time to offer reassurance of God's love.

Restlessness

As circulation and metabolism in the body slows, the person may experience involuntary motions and restlessness. Lightly massaging the hand or feet, as long as it does not cause pain, may help to calm the patient. Soft music playing in the background may also help.

Disorientation

At times, the person may seem confused and not recognize people around him/her. If the person doesn't recognize you, tell him your name. It is normal for a person nearing death to talk about seeing people who have already died. While we can't understand this completely, many speculate that it is a transitional time when the person is beginning a normal detachment from this life. The person should be allowed to freely talk about what he/she is experiencing. It is important to listen with respect and offer calm reassurance.

During my grandmother's final days she spoke of seeing her mother who had passed away over forty years before. One of her last visions was of Jesus waiting for her by the water. What she saw was very calming to her.

Incontinence

As muscles begin to relax, the person may lose control of urine and bowels. This can be very embarassing to the patient. Diapers or chux may be helpful to keep the person clean and comfortable.

Urine Decrease

Changes in urine near the end of life come about because of decreased fluid intake and a lessening of circulation through the kidneys. Urine output becomes more concentrated and may become the color of tea. A Foley catheter may be inserted to keep the bladder empty.

Breathing Pattern Change

Due to decreased circulation in the internal organs and buildup of body waste products, it is common for a person's breathing pattern to change near death. Breathing may become shallow, irregular, fast or abnormally slow. One pattern consists of breathing irregularly with shallow periods of no breaths for 5 to 30 seconds, followed by a deep breath. The person may also have periods of rapid breathing like panting. Sometimes air passing over relaxed vocal cords makes a moaning like sound.

Congestion

Oral secretions may become more profuse and collect in the back of the throat. The person may develop gurgling sounds from the chest. The sounds may become loud and distressing to hear. These normal changes come from fluid imbalance and an inability to cough up normal secretions.

Color Changes

The person's arms and legs may become cold, hot or discolored due to changes in circulation. Extremities may become a darker bluish hue. This is a normal indication that the circulation is conserving to the core to support the most vital organs. Irregular temperatures can be the result of the brain sending unclear messages. If the person sweats an odor may result from the physiological changes taking place.

Permission to Go

When someone enters the last days of dying, their body begins the process of shutting down, which will end when all the physical systems cease to function. This is usually an orderly and non-dramatic series of physical changes that are not medical emergencies and do not require invasive interventions. These changes are a normal, natural way in which the body prepares itself to die. This release may include resolving whatever is unfinished, and seeking or receiving permission from family members to "let go." A dying person will commonly try to hold on, even though it brings prolonged discomfort, in order to be assured that those left behind will be all right. A family's ability to reassure and release the dying person from this concern is the greatest gift of love they can give at this time.

Saying Goodbye

When the person is ready to die and the family is ready to let go this is the time to say good-bye in personal ways. It is a good time to hold the person's hand and say what needs to be said. The family is given the opportunity to say goodbye. This is a gift that not everyone is given. The final goodbye may be tearful. Tears are a normal and natural part of saying good-bye. Tears express your love and help you to let go.

During my grandmother's final days, we were given the gift of saying good-bye. My goodbye left nothing unsaid between us. It was a time when our hearts were open and we shared the most wonderful, personal time two people can have. It is special when you know for sure that your loved one is a child of God and is going home to be with the Lord. We will be together again. When a family member is near the end, they will try to hold on to life for their loved ones. When the family comes to grips with the imminent end and tells the person that it is OK to let go, the loved one can peacefully slip away. I'm not saying that the person will not die until they are told it's ok, but it will allow them to calmly and peacefully give in and let go.

At the Time of Death

It may be helpful for the family to discuss ahead of time what to do when the final moment arrives. At the time of death: breathing ceases, heartbeat ceases, the person cannot be aroused, the eyelids may be partially open with the eyes in a fixed stare, the mouth may fall open as the jaw relaxes, there is sometimes a release of bowel and bladder contents as the body relaxes.

If the person is under Hospice care the death is not an emergency. Hospice should be contacted at the time of death. There is no need to call 911 or the medical examiner. Hospice will have all the information on hand as to who should be called. When my grandmother passed away, I held a short bedside service with the close family that was present. We had prayer and scripture reading. It was a time when we comforted each other in our loss. My mother and I shared in preparing the body to be removed by the undertaker.

I chose to include these signs of how the body prepares for the final days to help the pastor know what to expect. I firmly believe that the pastor, as a spiritual caregiver, must play a large part in the care of the terminally ill. The pastor should know what to expect when he walks into a patient's room.

CHAPTER EIGHT

MINISTRY TO CHILDREN

MINISTRY TO CHILDREN

I worked the pediatric unit of a major government hospital in my CPE program. It is a special privilege to minister to sick children. They can teach us all something when it comes to faith.

Many churches have a Minister of Children and Youth. This is a real asset when it comes to ministering to the sick. It is important for the child to know and be comfortable with the person who ministers to them. Sunday school teachers are also a real help in this ministry. The wise Sunday school teacher will have built relationships with the children in their class.

When a teacher receives word that a child is ill, he/she should not delay in acting. If a call comes from someone other than a family member, the teacher should contact the family to get the facts. Many times stories spread throughout the church and facts are replaced by embellishments. The teacher/pastor should reassure the family of their caring, love and support. The teacher/pastor should write down all the information so that no misunderstandings will occur.

If the child has been taken to the ER because of sudden illness or injury, a pastoral care member should be present. This should be the Sunday school teacher, deacon or pastor. It is best that the child knows and trusts the person who goes. A child who has never had contact with the deacon and who does not know him personally will not feel comfortable with him. This may be a time of anxiety for both the patient and parent. Do not add to their anxiety.

It is helpful to get on the same level with the child. I have found that knowing a bit about what interests children can help break the ice. For instance, if you walk into a hospital room and the child is watching something on TV or a movie, it helps to know what it is. The pastor or teacher can use that as an ice-breaker to start a conversation with the child. Once the ice is broken then the pastor can make the child feel comfortable enough to talk. Not all children need or want to talk. Some children are shy and trying to force them into conversation, especially when sick, will only make things worse.

The pastor will spend much of his time during the visit talking to the parents. Parents have a tendency to want to speak for their children. They should not speak about the child as if he/she is not in the room. If the discussion is emotional or of a nature that the child should not hear, then it would be appropriate to ask the parents to talk to you in another room. Most hospitals have a conference area where the door can be shut to ensure privacy.

Just how much the child should be told about his/her illness can be the cause of stress and anxiety. The information given should always be age appropriate. It would serve no purpose to try to explain to a 3 year old that he has cancer. It could ruin the relationship a 17 year old has with his/her parents if he/she was not told the truth. The age and emotional stability are major factors in making the determination. The parents should have enough knowledge about the illness/injury to answer any questions the patient may have. In the case of an older child, it would be beneficial to have the doctor present to answer questions.

Children often ask why they are sick and doesn't God love them. Children can be told that being sick or having bad things happen is part of life, but God is big and strong and He loves them. They should be told that God doesn't want them to be sick and He didn't cause it. You can tell them that Jesus is with them and that they can pray and ask Him to help them get better. It is important that the child be reassured that God does love him/her and that God wants what is best. They need to trust in God even though they don't understand what is happening.

It can be difficult to determine the emotions of a child. If the pastor or Sunday school teacher visits the child, he/she may ask the child to draw a picture about how they feel or simply ask the child to talk to them. Children often don't know how to express themselves in words but when asked to draw a picture they can express themselves. This will give the pastoral care provider an idea about how the child is doing emotionally and spiritually. You can also explain to them how God has given gifts to the doctors and nurses and has sent them to help the child. This is a good time to explain how God uses others to help us when we need it. It can be a valuable teaching moment. A child who express that he/she is afraid can be reassured and it's an opening to share with them scripture that God is with them through everything. Fear is a normal emotion for a child who does not understand what is happening and when his/her daily routine is interrupted. Children don't know how to deal with emotions. Children who don't understand what is going on may respond in acting out in anger. Some children will go into denial. Allowing the child to express themselves in art or play can be a valuable too to determining the emotional state of the child.

Chronic and Life-Threatening Illnesses

The life of a child and his/her family can be turned upside down at the diagnosis of a life-threatening or chronic illness. The greatest fear of a parent is the death of a child. During the time of diagnosis the parent is faced with the reality that the child is ill and what they fear most may become reality. This can cause tremendous stress within the family. This is a time when families need to be ministered to and need to pull together. I know; I have been there. My son was diagnosed with cancer at the age of nineteen and if my husband and I were not strong Christians with the support of our pastor and Christian friends, I don't know how we would have made it.

When making a hospital visit to a child with a chronic or life-threatening illness, deal directly with the child. I like to take a small toy, such as a stuffed animal, for the child. Knowing some age appropriate toys, cartoons or videos can help you relate more easily to the child. It can sometimes be a way to break the ice with a little one. One of my patients was a three-year-old boy. He was very quiet and the mom said he wouldn't talk to me. The little boy was watching a cartoon on TV when I entered his room. Fortunately, I recognized the cartoon and was able to communicate with the patient about the cartoon. We then moved the conversation to his slippers, which had a different cartoon character on them. He made a game out of my guessing who was on the slippers. Within a few minutes time the patient had warmed to me. I visited the patient many times since he was in the hospital for several weeks. There were many opportunities to read Bible stories to him and tell him about Jesus' love.

Long hospitalizations of chronically ill children are very stressful on families and marriages. Parents need to realize this and work at keeping their marriage together. It takes a lot of time and energy when your child is sick. It takes even more time and energy when the child is hospitalized. It can be a very stressful time for the entire family. Couples may be separated for long periods of time and emotions are high. Some marriages do not survive the life threatening illness of a child. Some ways to help deal with this extremely stressful time, include the following:

- Share medical decisions
- Take turns staying at the hospital with the sick child
- Share responsibilities at home
- Seek counseling
- Accept that your spouse may cope differently[15]

When Jeremy was fighting cancer he was in and out of the hospital. He was nineteen and newly married. They had planned on starting their family as soon as they could and Kim became pregnant

3 months into the marriage. Then Jeremy was diagnosed with Testicular cancer. Our family was devastated. The cancer had metastasized and was very advanced. His wife had to hold her job for the health insurance. We had to pull together as a family to get through this time, and we did it but not alone. We took turns staying with Jeremy through the night while he was hospitalized. That may sound strange for a nineteen-year old but given what he was going through we gladly did it. There were times when I was so tired that I didn't think I could make it another day. Then my husband would stay and go home at six in the morning to get ready for work. On days when I just didn't feel up to cooking, a friend would somehow know and show up at the door with dinner.

During times when a child is sick, the parents are under tremendous stress. In our case, we not only had a sick son, but his pregnant wife and another son to care for. It can take a toll on families. The important thing is to communicate. As a pastor you will

---

[15] Janes-Hodder and Nancy Keene. **Childhood Cancer: A Parents Guide to Solid Tumor Cancers.** 2001, Patient Centered Guides.

encounter families going through similar situations. Counsel them to talk to each other. They need to express their feelings and fears. They need to pray together. This can be a time that really tests faith.

James 1:2-4

My brethren, count it all joy when ye fall into divers temptations; [3] Knowing this, that the trying of your faith worketh patience. [4] But let patience have her perfect work, that ye may be perfect and entire, wanting nothing.

Going through an experience like this can build your faith. Counsel your flock to turn their fears over to the Lord and rely on Him. That is really the only way to get through something like this. As parents, we expect to live longer than our children. When a child has a life threatening illness, it rocks our foundation and can cause us to have doubts. I have found that like patients, parents of children with life threatening or chronic illness will either draw closer to God or run in the other direction. The pastor needs to stay close and minister to the parents during this time.

The Family and Medical Leave Act

In some families both parents work and this can be a source of additional stress. The child may require that a parent be with him/her around the clock. This may cause financial problems and the parents may fear the loss of their jobs. Hospitals generally have social workers to help the parents in this area but it is good for the pastor to have some knowledge. The Family and Medical Leave Act (FMLA) is intended to provide a means for employees to balance their work and family responsibilities by taking unpaid leave for certain reasons. The Act is intended to promote both the stability and economic security of families, and the national interests in preserving family integrity. The FMLA is applicable to any employer in the private sector who is engaged in commerce or in any industry or activity affecting commerce, and who has 50 or more employees each working day during at least 20 calendar weeks or more in the current or preceding calendar year.

All public agencies (state and local government) and local education agencies (schools) are covered. These employers do not need to meet the 50 employee test. Most federal employees are covered by Title II of FMLA and are subject to regulations issued by the Office of Personnel Management. In order to be "eligible" for FMLA leave, an employee must be employed by a covered employer and work at a worksite within 75 miles of which that employer employs at least 50 employees; must have worked at least 12 months (which do not have to be consecutive) for the employer; and, must have worked at least 1,250 hours during the 12 months immediately preceding the date of commencement of FMLA leave.

Basic Provisions/Requirements

The FMLA provides an entitlement of up to 12 weeks of job-protected, unpaid leave during any 12 months for the following reasons:

- Birth and care of the employee's child or placement for adoption or foster care of a child with the employee.
- To care for an immediate family member (spouse, child, parent) who has a serious health condition; or

- For the employee's own serious health condition.

An employer must maintain group health benefits that an employee was receiving at the time leave began during periods of FMLA leave at the same level and in the same manner as if the employee had continued to work. Under most circumstances, an employee may elect or the employer may require the use of any accrued paid leave (vacation, sick, personal, etc.) for periods of unpaid FMLA leave. FMLA leave may be taken in blocks of time less than the full 12 weeks on an intermittent or reduced leave basis.[16]

The church can play a vital role in helping parents when the child needs care. A team of caregivers can coordinate times when someone can relieve the parent to get some rest or do some errands. Church members can also be on hand to run errands or bring in food. When both parents work it can be stressful, but it can be just as stressful in single parent families or when one parent doesn't work outside the home. The illness of a child is just plain stressful. A pastor who knows this and approaches the family with Christ's love and tangible ways in which the church can help is truly a man of God.

Care of the Terminally Ill Child

When a child is dying care turns from cure to comfort. The child should be spared invasive painful procedures and be afforded the same comfort measures as an adult. The following guidelines are given by the University of Utah Health Sciences Center in caring for the needs of the dying child.[17]

- **A routine for sleep and rest.** The terminally ill child will need to have adequate time for rest and sleep. The pastor is advised to call before visiting the child and parents.

- **Nutrition considerations.** Nutritional considerations for the dying child may be difficult to address. Nausea, vomiting, diarrhea, and reduced eating are often associated with the effects of treatment and the progression of the disease.

---

[16] **The Family and Medical Leave Act of 1993.** Public law 103-3 enacted February 5, 1993.

Artificial nutrition and hydration are covered elsewhere in this course. The decision on when and if to begin artificial nutrition and hydration can be very difficult for the parents. This is a time when the parents may seek counsel and support from the pastor.

- **Changes in elimination.** Diarrhea, constipation, and incontinence are all possible with the dying child. Care should be given to keep the child clean. It is important to not embarrass the child who is unable to control these bodily functions.

- **Respiratory changes.** Respiratory changes may occur from pneumonia, medication or from the disease itself. Often, the child will feel as though they can't catch their breath. This can be very freightening to a child. Oxygen supplied through the nose of mask may be needed for comfort.

---

[17] **Care of the Terminally Ill Child.** University of Utah Health Sciences Center.

- **Pain management.** Pain management is important with the dying child. One of the dying child's greatest fears is pain. The ultimate goal is comfort and all appropriate measures should be taken to assure the child is free from pain. Addiction to pain medication should not be a concern with a dying child.

Methods for reducing pain are classified as either pharmacological or non-pharmacological. Pharmacological pain management refers to the use of pharmaceutical drugs or medications to relieve pain. There are many types of drugs and several methods used in administering them. Pain medication is usually given in one of following ways:

- Orally
- Intravenously, IV
- Using a special catheter
- Through a patch on the skin

Examples of **pharmacological** pain relief include the following:

- Analgesics (mild pain relievers)
- Sedation (usually given by IV)
- Anesthesia (usually given by IV)
- Topical anesthetics (cream put on the skin to numb the area)
- Pain relievers

Examples of **non-pharmacological** pain management:

- Psychological
    - Explain procedures in detail using pictures if necessary.
    - Allow the child time to ask the doctor questions.
    - Give the child a tour of the room where the procedure will take place.
    - Adolescents may view a tape of the procedure, while small children may play the procedure on a doll.
- Imagery. Guide a child through an imaginary mental image of sights, sounds, tastes, smells, and feelings to shift attention away from the pain.
- Prayer. Prayer can help relieve pain, fears, and uncertainty.

- Distraction. Distraction can be helpful with babies by using colorful, moving objects. Singing songs, telling stories, or looking at books or videos can distract preschoolers. Older children may watch TV or listen to music as a distraction.

- Relaxation. Children can be guided through relaxation exercises such as deep breathing and stretching, to reduce discomfort.[18]

Siblings of Sick Children

When a child has a life threatening illness the entire family is affected. The siblings of the sick child present an opportunity for ministry. This can be a very frightening and confusing time for them. Especially young children can become very emotional and fearful. Jealousy and resentment can also surface in the sibling. As a pastor, it is an area in which counsel should be given to the parents as well as the child. Many parents are so caught up in the illness of the sick child that they don't think about how it is affecting the healthy ones. Parents may have regrets and guilt for years about things they didn't do for or with the healthy child. I am presenting this section so the pastor can be better informed about what the family is experiencing during the time of a child's illness.

When my son was diagnosed with cancer, our family was turned upside down. My youngest was a senior in high school. We were home schooling and I was his primary teacher. There were times when I would have to give him assignments for several days while I stayed at the hospital. Sometimes I took him along but it was not an environment that was conducive to learning. It was a real struggle for both of us because I felt bad about neglecting him, yet I had to be there for my other son. Our pastor was very supportive. Our church was very supportive. Church members were there when Nick needed help with anything. I have regrets about that time and about things Nick missed. He didn't get to go visit colleges like we had planned. He settled for the local community college. He had dreams of becoming an Archaeologist, which were put on hold. I found out several years later that he was very depressed during this time. I feel

---

[18] **Care of the Terminally Ill Child.** University of Utah Health Services Center.

guilt over not seeing that and getting him help and spending more time with him. I believe that an observant pastor may spot things that he can bring out to help the sibling. There are many emotions, which may arise during this time.

The following information is extracted from **Childhood Cancer: A Parent's Guide to Solid Tumor Cancers**, by Honna Janes-Hodder and Nancy Keene.[19] Concern is an obvious emotion. We are all concerned when someone we love is sick. When a child's brother or sister is sick this concern can easily turn to fear. They may feel that they too may become sick. They may feel vulnerable and afraid. The child may fear the death of the sibling, or they may fear their own death. Parents need to talk to the child honestly in age-appropriate terms. Pastors can help when the child has spiritual concerns.

Jealousy is another emotion that can emerge when a sibling is ill. Parents spend most of their time with the sick child, and are often at the hospital. Visitors often bring a present to the sick but not to the healthy child. Phone calls and conversations often revolve around the sick. With all the attention focused on the sick child it is only natural that the healthy one would become jealous.

Siblings often feel guilty when their brother or sister is sick. Children feel the world revolves around them so if someone is sick, it must be his/her fault. At times when children squabble they say things like, "I hope you die." Then when the child does get sick they fear death as a result of their wish. The child should be assured early in the illness that it is not the result of anything they have done. They need to be told repeatedly throughout the illness that it isn't their fault. Feelings of guilt can also come from the fact that the sibling is sick but they are healthy. They may also feel guilty over their emotions, such as jealousy or anger. Parents need to talk to the healthy child and get them to express how they are feeling and get their emotions out.

---

[19] Janes-Hodder and Nancy Keene. **Childhood Cancer: A Parent's Guide to Solid Tumor Cancers.** 2001, Patient Centered Guides.

Children often feel sad and abandoned when their brother or sister is hospitalized. When the parents spend time away with the sick child, the healthy child is often sent to a relative or someone comes into the home to watch them. This can make the child feel as though he/she is not part of the family. They can feel abandoned. As much as possible at least one of the parents should be with the healthy child. Again, it is important to get the child to share what he/she is feeling. Keeping the thoughts and emotions bottled up can cause much pain in the present and problems for them in the future. The sadness a healthy child feels can be a combination of many things. The sadness can be a manifested in crying, withdrawal, behavior problems, or in other ways.

Anger is another emotion that arises from the situation of a sick sibling. Children don't like it when their lives are turned upside down. They like stability, we all do. The healthy child may become angry when left with a sitter. They may feel they aren't getting the attention they should. This can bring out anger that makes tempers flare. Parents need to remember that when they are with the healthy child, they need to give them their full attention. Half listening to what the child is saying will only cause more anger.

Children worry about what happens when the sibling goes to the hospital. If possible, take the healthy child for a visit and let them see what is happening. I may put to rest some of their fears. They may have seen scenes on TV that have stuck in their minds and the imagination has taken over, leading them to believe the worst about the sibling. Allowing the child to visit gives them a chance to see for themselves what is happening. Many hospitals have videos the child can watch that will show procedures and discuss hospital routines. Age-appropriate books are available to help also. Just being with the sibling can bring to rest worries and be comforting to both the sick and healthy child.

Helping Siblings Cope[20]

- Explain the illness and its treatment to the siblings in terms that they understand. Encourage them to ask questions. Make a list of the questions that you can't answer and take them

[20] Ibid

with you to ask the doctor, or offer to let the child go along to ask the question himself/herself.

- Make them understand that nothing they did caused the illness. If the child is not contagious, make them understand that they will not get it from being around the sibling.
- Try to spend time alone with the siblings.
- If possible, use a tape recorder to send messages back and forth between the siblings, or allow them to talk on the phone.
- Share your feelings with the healthy child.
- Include the healthy child in decision making and make sure they feel that they are a part of the family.
- Give lots of hugs and kisses.
- Alert the healthy child's teacher about what is happening at home. The healthy child will have emotional times as noted above and the teacher needs to be aware.
- To help with feelings of jealousy, encourage the sick child to share the gifts he/she receives and reward the healthy child as much as possible.

- Encourage a close relative or friend to become close to the healthy child so they will have someone to make him/her feel special and hopefully open up to.
- Seek a support group for the healthy child so they will have others to talk to who are experiencing the same thing.

Scripture to read to the child in sickness and when they are afraid. I generally use the NIV version because it is easily understood by the children.

Psalm 73:23

Yet I am always with you; you hold me by my right hand. (NIV)

1 Peter 5:7

Cast all your anxiety on him because he cares for you. (NIV)

Psalm 56:3

When I am afraid, I will trust in you. (NIV)

John 14:27

Peace I leave with you; my peace I give you. I do not give to you as the world gives. Do not let your hearts be troubled and do not be afraid. (NIV)

Hebrews 13:6

So we may say with confidence, The Lord *is* my helper; I will not be afraid. What can man do to me? (NIV)

Psalm 46:1

God *is* our refuge and strength, an ever present help in trouble. (NIV)

Accidents

This same approach should be taken in dealing with children when there is an accident or illness in the family. They need reassurance that, they are loved by God, and that He is watching over them. They also need to know that there will be times when people get sick or hurt, but that God doesn't make that happen to them. They need to know that these things are part of life. They also need to know that they can put their trust and faith in God.

Accidents are the leading cause of death in children and cancer is second. In 1998 a study was done of the families of the children who had died of cancer and had received their care at the Dana-Farber Cancer Institute or the Children's Hospital in Boston, MA. One hundred three parents were interviewed. Almost 80% of the children died of progressive disease and the rest died of treatment-related complications. Forty-nine percent of the children died in the hospital, half of those in the intensive care unit. Eighty-nine percent suffered a great deal from at least on symptom in their last month. Suffering from pain was more likely in children whose parents reported that the physician was not actively involved in providing end-of-life care. The study concluded that children who die of cancer receive aggressive treatment at the end of life. Many have substantial suffering in the last month of life, and attempts to control their symptoms are often unsuccessful. Greater attention must be paid to palliative care for children who are dying of cancer.[21]

What are the ethical considerations when a baby or child is terminal and artificial nourishment is the only way to keep the child alive? The Child Abuse Ammendments of 1984 mandate that "medically indicated treatment" cannot be withheld-"including *appropriate* nutrition, hydration, and medication"-if "in the treating physician's *reasonable* medical judgment it will be most likely to be effective in ameliorating or correcting all of an infant's life-threatening conditions.

Expectations to the requirement to provide treatment exist when:

- "The infant is chronically and irreversibly comatose; or the provision of treatment would merely prolong dying, or would not be effective in ameliorating or correcting all the life threatening conditions, or otherwise be futile in terms of

[21] "Symptoms and suffering at the end of life in children with cancer." Wolfe J, et.al. New England Journal of Medicine, 2000 February 3;342(5):326-33.

survival; or the provision of such treatment would be virtually futile in terms of survival and the treatment itself under such circumstances would be *inhumane*."[22]

Although the amendment applies to infants up to the age of one year, there is reason to think that they have implications for all children with handicapping conditions.

In the above, it states *appropriate* nutrition. That means what is appropriate for the situation. It means, will the treatment work for this condition in this child? Artificial feedings can cause harm. IV's for hydration means repeated needle sticks and discomfort. Insertion of a catheter may mean infection or complications. Withholding artificial feeding does not mean the child will suffer.

Reasonable means that the judgment must be carefully thought through. Each child and each case is different and must be thought through. For example, feeding a brain-damaged child with no gag reflex could lead to aspiration.

---

[22] Federal Register, April 15, 1985: 14878).

Inhumane is the term used by some when the decision is made to not start artificial feeding and hydration. Infants who were not hydrated but were provided with adequate sedation and comfort care appear to not suffer. [23]

[23] Ethicscope, Fall 1993. Childrens National Medical Center. P. 3.

CHAPTER NINE

SPIRITUAL NEEDS ASSESSMENT

Spiritual Needs Assessment

In order for the pastor to assess the spiritual needs of the patient, he must be observant and tuned in to the patient's response. The pastor has the advantage of knowing the person and having that person's respect. This will generally allow the pastor to minister more effectively to the needs.

George Fitchett in **Assessing Spiritual Needs: A Guide for Caregivers**, has identified nine characteristic features of approaches to spiritual assessment.

1. *Implicit assessment.* This is one of the most common forms of assessment in pastoral care. This assessment is not stated but merely implied.
2. *Inspired assessment.* Inspired pastoral actions come from divine revelation. This type of assessment comes to the pastor when, not knowing what to say or pray, the words come to him from the

Lord. This divine inspiration can also come to the caregiver. The caregiver could be inspired to call for the elders of the church to come to the bedside and annoint the sick with oil.

3. *Intuitive assessment.* At times the pastor will be guided by intuition as a feeling or sensation. The pastor may get a gut feeling.
4. *Idiosyncratic assessment.* These assessments are derived from the gifts and knowledge of the caregiver. These assessments aren't shared with others. It is considered an ad hoc diagnostic schema.
5. *Assessments based on Traditional Pastoral Acts.* Most pastoral assessments come from pastoral actions that are traditionally expected in a specific life situation. Faith groups have their own traditions. Catholics call for the priest when a person is nearing death. Protestant pastors will visit and pray orally with the sick or bereaved. Pastors traditionally help individuals accept the pain of bereavement by encouraging the expression of grief.
6. *Assessment based on Normative Pastoral Stances.* For some pastors, the approach to assessment focuses on the attitude or stance rather than on behavior or on the explicit need of the patient. What is important is that the pastor "be present", to "be

available", to "be empathetic", to "be authentic", or to "offer hospitality".

7. *Global Assessment.* Pastors may use one or two broad diagnostic categories when making pastoral assessments. For example, if the patient is lonely and anxious, the pastor may believe it is important to be cheerful and encouraging.
8. *Psychological assessment.* Some pastors may think diagnostically in making their assessment. They may do so in using psychiatric categories or language.
9. *Explicit Spiritual Assessment.* Sometimes the pastoral care is based on a purely spiritual assessment of what the person needs or what the situation calls for. [24]

What is Spiritual Assessment? Spiritual is the dimension of life that reflects the need to find meaning in existence and in which we respond to the sacred. Assessment is the information gathering and interpreting process that leads to the diagnosis. The assessment process involves both objective and interpretive aspects.

A pastor who knows the sick member will have certain advantages. He will generally know the commitment level and may be able to assess the patient more easily. He should never, however, assume to know what the patient needs. The pastor may inquire of the patient, how they may minister to their needs. The pastor may also assess the situation and meet the needs as he sees them. He may have been in a similar situation, or ministered to others with the same illness, but each individual is unique and ministry to the person should be unique. During lengthy or chronic illnesses, the pastor should continually reevaluate the patient's needs. The patient will go through different emotions and the pastor will need to be aware of where the person is spiritually and emotionally.

The question is often asked, "Why do an assessment?" The spiritual assessment can give us a good idea about the direction that our ministry should take. It will help us to set goals that we can strive

---

[24] Fritchett, George. Assessing Spiritual Needs: A Guide for Caregivers. Augsburg Press, 1993.

to achieve in our ministry. The assessment will give the pastor a clue to the matters that most concern the sick. Then the pastor will be better able to understand the patient and help him/her.

Pastors will develop their own style of Spiritual assessment through experience. I have personally found that by exploring a person's beliefs I can get an idea of what they believe is the meaning and purpose of their life. Christians, for example, state that they are children of God and that gives their life meaning. Not all will be able to articulate what they feel is the purpose and meaning of life. Many times the pastor will pick this up through conversation. The pastor needs to tune in to key words and phrases. Listen to what the person is saying about what is important in their life. It could be something or someone in their family, or it could be a religious symbol or act. A mother, for example, may feel that the meaning to her life is raising her children. You need to key in to what the person views as important. Observing the actions and the direction the patient moves the conversation can also give clues that will help in the assessment. Verbal clues may come in the form of speaking about God or a higher power. The patient may talk about prayer, church, or a spiritual leader. Sometimes the patient will comment that, "It's all in God's hands now!" or "Why is God allowing this to happen?" Listen for these key words and you will gain much insight into the spiritual state of the patient.

The pastor should also look for visual clues that will aid in his assessment. A quick glance around the room can offer much. Take special notice of a Bible or spiritual books that are visible. These can give you a starting point for talking to the patient. You can say something as simple as, "I see your Bible, is there anything special that you would like for me to read to you?" Often this will lead the patient into discussing where they are spiritually. When one faces imminent death one feels an urgency to examine their life.

The pastor also needs to key into the duties and obligations a person feels he/she needs to fulfill. These may be duties they feel they need to perform for their families. A man who is sick and unable to work may feel guilt for not providing for his family. A person may feel that these duties add meaning to his/her life. Loss of the ability to perform their duties and meet their obligations may make people feel that life now has no meaning or that they are letting others down. The pastor must be sensitive to the situation of the sick. This is an important part of the spiritual assessment.

The pastor should also assess the emotional tone of the sick person. There will generally be an underlying emotion, whether anger, fear, or some other emotion. The sick will also experience changes in emotions. When diagnosed with a major disease, such as cancer, a person may initially be shocked, followed by denial, anger or fear. The patient will go through an array of emotions during an illness. The pastor can ask the patient about their emotions but must also watch for clues so they won't miss any underlying emotions that need to be dealt with. For example, when my son was diagnosed with cancer, he went through many emotions. At one point he blamed me for his cancer, but the underlying emotion was fear. When we were able to deal with his fear, we found that the anger subsided. A patient can also be feeling anxiety yet cover it up by a sense of peacefulness.

The pastor must watch for clues that the patient is experiencing spiritual distress. He must be on the lookout for severe depression and suicidal ideation. Some who are suffering fall into depression and want to give up. The pastor should also learn to pick up on any feelings of abandonment by God, or feelings of anger toward God. Be especially watchful for signs of loss of hope. The pastor who learns to make a good spiritual assessment of the sick will be much more affective in ministering to the needs.

Another aspect of assessment is spiritual growth. The pastor should assess how the patient is growing spiritually through the illness. Is the person calling upon God? Is the person showing courage in fighting the illness? It has been my experience that a person will either move closer to God or move away from God during a major illness. Sometimes, a person will question God, question His whereabouts in the time when they need Him. Many will find this a time to seek answers to their questions about God. Many will take this time to open the Door and let the Lord enter. The pastor can make this assessment by listening to the patient and openly discussing where he/she is and what they are feeling.

The pastor also needs to assess the person's life within the community. He should inquire if the patient is getting out, and if they are able to take part in normal activities. The pastor must be sensitive in this area. A bedfast person would obviously not be able to go to the church's skating party. But a general inquiry could be made. It is a good idea for churches to have something in place to minister to the sick. Church members could rotate taking meals to the family and visiting. This can be very uplifting to the sick. It's a good idea to have this in place before it is needed. It is also good to have a plan so that no one is missed and feelings aren't hurt. A tape ministry can be uplifting to a homebound person. A tape of the Sunday service can be delivered to the member along with a bulletin from the service. It's also nice to keep the member current with Sunday school literature. Don't forget the member who is sick or homebound.

In the assessment, the pastor should also seek the approval of the patient to continue care. This should be done verbally. If the patient says they would like for you to visit again, then the pastor should tell them when the next visit will likely be. It is advisable for the pastor to have specific times set aside for pastoral care of the congregation. In a crisis situation this isn't possible. But for routine visits to the chronically ill or dying, it is good to set up specific times that will fit the treatment schedule of the patient and the busy schedule of the pastor. Always assure the person that in an emergency you are available. When you set up a time to return, keep it unless an emergency arises. Many times an ill person who looks forward to the pastor's visit will become saddened and depressed if they feel let down when the pastor doesn't show up. They need to know that they are important to you and to God.

SPIRITUAL ASSESSMENT

Listen for verbal cues:

- Patient refers to God
- Patient talks about prayer or church
- Patient makes comments such as, "It's all in God's hands now."

Look for Visual cues:

- Bible or other spiritual books

- Symbols such as the cross
- Articles such as pins or tracts

SPIRITUAL DIAGNOSIS

Cues that the patient may be experiencing spiritual distress/despair:

- Anticipatory grief
- Inability to participate in religious practice
- Severe depression, suicidal ideation
- Concern about relationship with God
- Feeling abandoned by God
- Anger toward God
- Loss of hope

INTERVENTIONS

- Pray or read scripture with patient
- Be with patient in respectful silence

Listen carefully to the patient's life story: who they are, who they have been, for this is the key to understanding their unique spirituality.

CHAPTER TEN

HIV/AIDS

HIV/AIDS

A disease that carries much stigma is AIDS. I worked in a clinic with pediatric HIV/AIDS patients and ministered to the parents, as well as, the adults. I was very distressed to hear from two mothers that the pastor of their church informed them that they were not to return when they were told the child had HIV. I think a lot of the fear comes from ignorance of what HIV/AIDS is and how it can spread. As a pastor you will probably be faced with a member sooner or later who has contracted HIV. Like any other life threatening disease, the sick person needs spiritual care as part of their treatment. It can be at this time that the person is really seeking God and the love shown in HIS name will reap rewards. It is a true blessing to minister to the sick and to hold the hand of a dying child and tell them of Jesus' love. The church community is faced with a unique challenge in dealing with the AIDS population. This challenge comes from not only the nature of the disease and how it was acquired but in the fact that there is no cure.

I am including this section on HIV/AIDS to inform the pastor and pastoral care worker about this dreaded disease that is in epidemic proportions worldwide. The information furnished in this section comes from the National Institute of Allergy and Infectious Diseases (NIAIDS) of the National Institute of Health and from the Centers for Disease Control and Prevention (CDC).

HIV Infection and AIDS: An Overview

AIDS-acquired immunodeficiency syndrome- was first reported in the United States in 1981 and is now a worldwide epidemic. The Human Immunodeficiency Virus (HIV) causes AIDS. HIV progressively destroys the body's ability to fight infections and certain cancers by killing or damaging cells of the body's immune system. Those diagnosed with AIDS may get life threatening diseases called opportunistic infections, which are caused by microbes such as viruses or bacteria that usually don't make healthy people sick.

More than 700,000 cases of AIDS have been reported in the United States since 1981, and as many as 900,000 Americans may be infected with HIV. The epidemic is growing most rapidly among minority populations and is the leading killer of African-American males. According to the U.S. Centers for Disease Control and Prevention (CDC), AIDS affects nearly seven times more African Americans than whites and three times more Hispanics than whites.[25]

How HIV Causes AIDS

A significant component of the research effort of the National Institute of Allergy and Infectious Diseases (NIAID) is devoted to the pathogenesis of human immunodeficiency virus (HIV) disease. Studies on pathogenesis address the complex mechanisms that result in the destruction of the immune system of an HIV-infected person. A detailed understanding of HIV and how it establishes infection and causes the acquired immunodeficiency syndrome (AIDS) is crucial to identifying and developing effective drugs and vaccines to fight HIV and AIDS. This fact sheet summarizes the state of knowledge in this area and provides a brief glossary of terms.

---

[25] CDC *HIV/AIDS Surveillance Report*, Vol. 12. 2000.

Overview

HIV disease is characterized by a gradual deterioration of immune function. Most notably, crucial immune cells called CD4+ T cells are disabled and killed during the typical course of infection. These cells, sometimes called "T-helper cells," play a central role in the immune response, signaling other cells in the immune system to perform their special functions.

A healthy, uninfected person usually has 800 to 1,200 CD4+ T cells per cubic millimeter (mm3) of blood. During HIV infection, the number of these cells in a person's blood progressively declines. When a person's CD4+ T cell count falls below 200/mm3, he or she becomes particularly vulnerable to the opportunistic infections and cancers that typify AIDS, the end stage of HIV disease. People with AIDS often suffer infections of the lungs, intestinal tract, brain, eyes and other organs, as well as debilitating weight loss, diarrhea, neurologic conditions and cancers such as Kaposi's sarcoma and certain types of lymphomas.

Most scientists think that HIV causes AIDS by directly inducing the death of CD4+ T cells or interfering with their normal function, and by triggering other events that weaken a person's immune function. For example, the network of signaling molecules that normally regulates a person's immune response is disrupted during HIV disease, impairing a person's ability to fight other infections. The HIV-mediated destruction of the lymph nodes and related immunologic organs also plays a major role in causing the immunosuppression seen in people with AIDS.

Scope of the HIV Epidemic

Although HIV was first identified in 1983, studies of previously stored blood samples indicate that the virus entered the U.S. population sometime in the late 1970s. In the United States, 774,467 cases of AIDS, and 448,060 deaths among people with AIDS had been reported to the Centers for Disease Control and Prevention (CDC) as of the end of 2000. Approximately 40,000 new HIV infections occur each year in the United States, 70 percent of them among men and 30 percent among women. Minority groups in the United States have been disproportionately affected by the epidemic.

- Worldwide, an estimated 36.1 million people (47 percent of whom are female) were living with HIV/AIDS as of December 2000, according to the Joint United Nations Programme on HIV/AIDS (UNAIDS).

- Through 2000, cumulative HIV/AIDS-associated deaths worldwide numbered approximately 21.8 million: 17.5 million adults and 4.3 million children younger than 15 years.

- Globally, approximately 5.3 million new HIV infections and 3.0 million HIV/AIDS-related deaths occurred in the year 2000 alone.

HIV is a Retrovirus

HIV belongs to a class of viruses called retroviruses. Retroviruses are ribonucleic acid (RNA) viruses, and in order to replicate they must make a deoxyribonucleic acid (DNA) copy of their RNA. It is the DNA genes that allow the virus to replicate.

Like all viruses, HIV can replicate only inside cells, commandeering the cell's machinery to reproduce. However, only HIV and other retroviruses, once inside a cell, use an enzyme called reverse transcriptase to convert their RNA into DNA, which can be incorporated into the host cell's genes.

Slow viruses.

HIV belongs to a subgroup of retroviruses known as lentiviruses, or "slow" viruses. The course of infection with these viruses is characterized by a long interval between initial infection and the onset of serious symptoms.

Other lentiviruses infect nonhuman species. For example, the feline immunodeficiency virus (FIV) infects cats and the simian immunodeficiency virus (SIV) infects monkeys and other nonhuman primates. Like HIV in humans, these animal viruses primarily infect immune system cells, often causing immunodeficiency and AIDS-like symptoms. These viruses and their hosts have provided researchers with useful, albeit imperfect, models of the HIV disease process in people.

Transmission of HIV

Among adults, HIV is spread most commonly during sexual intercourse with an infected partner. During sex, the virus can enter the body through the mucosal linings of the vagina, vulva, penis, or rectum after intercourse or, rarely, via the mouth and possibly the upper gastrointestinal tract after oral sex. The likelihood of transmission is increased by factors that may damage these linings, especially other sexually transmitted diseases that cause ulcers or inflammation.

Research suggests that immune system cells of the dendritic cell type, which reside in the mucosa, may begin the infection process after sexual exposure by binding to and carrying the virus from the site of infection to the lymph nodes where other immune system cells become infected.

HIV also can be transmitted by contact with infected blood, most often by the sharing of needles or syringes contaminated with minute quantities of blood containing the virus. The risk of acquiring HIV from blood transfusions is now extremely small in the United States, as all blood products in this country are screened routinely for evidence of the virus.

Almost all HIV-infected children acquire the virus from their mothers before or during birth. In the United States, approximately 25 percent of pregnant HIV-infected women not receiving antiretroviral therapy have passed on the virus to their babies. The use of combinations of antiretroviral drugs has reduced the rate of mother-to-child (Vertically Acquired) HIV transmission in the United States. In developing countries, cheap and simple antiviral drug regimens have been proven to significantly reduce mother-to-child transmission in resource-poor settings The virus also may be transmitted from an HIV-infected mother to her infant via breastfeeding.[26]

HIV/AIDS cannot be transmitted by casual contact. It is ok to touch a person with AIDS. HIV/AIDS patients need to feel loved; you will not get AIDS from hugging them. The AIDS virus is fragile and cannot live outside the human host. It is not airborne and cannot be transmitted through hugging, kissing, or touching. Gloves are not needed for normal touch but should be worn when handling bodily fluids.

After years of following the spread of AIDS, researchers have found that it is no respecter of persons. AIDS touches all races, age groups, and nationalities.

HIV/AIDS Statistics

The National Institute of Allergy and Infectious Diseases (NIAID) is a reliable, current source of information on HIV/AIDS. The following information is from NIAID.[27]

---

[26] National Institutes of Allergy and Infectious Diseases. National Institute of Health, Bethesda, MD. *How HIV causes Aids.* 2001.

[27] National Institutes of Allergy and Infectious Diseases, National Institute of Health, Bethesda, MD. *HIV/AIDS Statistics Fact Sheet.* December 2001.

HIV/AIDS Worldwide

- As of the end of 2001, an estimated 40 million people worldwide-37.2 million adults and 2.7 million children younger than 15 years-were living with HIV/AIDS.

- Worldwide, approximately one in every 100 adults aged 15 to 49 is HIV infected.

- Approximately 48 percent of adults living with HIV/AIDS worldwide are women.

- An estimated 5 million new HIV infections offered worldwide during 2001; that is, about 14,000 infections each day.

- In 2001, approximately 6,000 young people aged 15 to 24 became infected with HIV every day-that is, about every five minutes.

- In 2001 alone, HIV/AIDS associated illnesses caused the deaths of approximately 3 million people worldwide, including an estimated 580,000 children younger than 15 years.

- Worldwide, more than 80 percent of all adult HIV infections have resulted from heterosexual intercourse.

HIV/AIDS in the United States

- The Centers for Disease Control and Prevention (CDC) estimate that 800,000 to 900,000 U.S. residents are living with HIV infection, one third of whom are unaware of their infection.

- Approximately 40,000 new HIV infections occur each year in the United States, about 70 percent among men and 30 percent among women. Of these newly infected people, half are younger than 25 years of age.

- Of new infections among men in the United States, the CDC estimates that approximately 60 percent of men were infected through homosexual sex, 25 percent through injection drug use, and 15 percent through heterosexual sex. Of newly infected men, approximately 50 percent are black, 30 percent are white, 20 percent are Hispanic, and a small percentage are members of other racial/ethnic groups.

- Of new infections among women in the United States, CDC estimates that approximates 75 percent of women were infected through heterosexual sex and 25 percent through injection drug use. Of newly infected women, approximately 64 percent are black, 18 percent are white, 18 percent are Hispanic, and a small percentage are from other racial/ethnic groups.

- In the United States, 774,467 cases of AIDS had been reported to the CDC through December 31, 2000.

- The estimated number of new adult/adolescent AIDS cases diagnosed in the United States was 49,691 in 1997, 42,955 in 1998, and 41,680 in 1999.

- In 2000, 41,960 new cases of AIDS in adults/adolescents were reported in the United States. In the same year, 196 new pediatric AIDS cases were reported.

- The rate of adult/adolescent AIDS cases reported in the United States in 2000 (per 100,000 population) was 74.2 among blacks, 30.4 among Hispanics, 12.7 among American Indians/Alaskan Natives, 7.9 among whites, and 4.3 among Asians/Pacific Islanders.

- From 1985 to 2000, the proportion of adult/adolescent AIDS cases in the United States reported in women increased from 7 percent to 25 percent.

- As of the end of 2000, an estimated 322,685 people in the United States were living with AIDS.

- As of December 31, 2000, 448,060 deaths among people with AIDS had been reported to the CDC. AIDS is now the fifth leading cause of death in the United States among people aged 25 to 44, and is the leading cause of death ffor black men in this age group. Among black women in this age group, HIV ranks third.

- The estimated annual number of AIDS-related deaths in the United States fell approximately 67 percent from 1995 to 1999, from 50,877 deaths in 1995 to 17,767 deaths in 1999.

- Of the estimated 16,767 AIDS-related deaths in the United States in 1999, approximately 50 percent were among blacks, 30 percent among whites, 18 percent among Hispanics, and less than 1 percent among Asians/Pacific Islanders and American Indians/Alaskan Natives.

As you can see from the statistics, HIV/AIDS is widespread, touching all age groups and nationalities. The preacher can help stop the spread of AIDS by preaching Scriptural truth from the altar. Many pastors shy away from preaching against homosexuality and sexual sins. During this time epidemics in sexually transmitted diseases, including HIV/AIDS, it is crucial that the pastor inform the church of what God has to say.

Leviticus 18:22

Thou shalt not lie with mankind, as with womankind: it is abomination.

Leviticus 20:13

If a man also lie with mankind, as he lieth with a woman, both of them have committed an abomination: they shall surely be put to death; their blood shall be upon them.

1 Cor. 6:9-10

Know ye not that the unrighteous shall not inherit the kingdom of God? Be not deceived: neither fornicators, nor idolaters, nor adulterers, nor effeminate, nor abusers of themselves with mankind, [10] Nor thieves, nor covetous, nor drunkards, nor revilers, nor extortioners, shall inherit the kingdom of God.

From these verses we can clearly see that homosexuality is detestable to God and is clearly a sin. It is also called an abomination and calls for death to both parties involved. Those committing the homosexual act will not inherit the kingdom of God.

Many liberal churches today preach from the pulpit that homosexuality is acceptable and that God made some to be homosexual. Some liberal denominations even ordain homosexuals and give them a flock to shepherd. This goes against God's plan. If God had intended for man to be with man and woman to be with woman the earth would have ceased to be populated many, many years ago. Instead, God gave us the example from the beginning of one man and one woman in marriage.

Genesis 2:20-24

And Adam gave names to all cattle, and to the fowl of the air, and to every beast of the field; but for Adam there was not found an help meet for him. [21] And the Lord God caused a deep sleep to fall upon Adam and he slept: and he took one of his ribs, and closed up the flesh instead thereof; [22] And the rib, which the Lord God had taken from man, made he a woman, and brought her unto the man. [23] And Adam said, This is now bone of my bones, and flesh of my flesh: she shall be called Woman, because she was taken out of Man. [24]

Therefore shall a man leave his father and his mother, and shall cleave unto his wife: and they shall be one flesh.

Isn't that wonderful. Woman was taken out of man. Husband and wife are to be of one flesh. No mention is made of God also making man and man of one flesh in marriage. There is no Scriptural foundation for same sex marriages.

Hospital Visits to the HIV/AIDS Patient

When the HIV/AIDS patient is hospitalized, the pastor needs to make every effort to visit. Often, the patient is ostracized by other patients. Precautions against infection must be taken. The patient is very vulnerable to infection and the pastor or pastoral care person should not enter the room if sick himself. AIDS patients are often starved for loved and need to be touched more than other patients. As with other patients, the pastor must listen, talk and touch. The ministry of presence is important to the AIDS patient.

In Ideas For Hospital Ministries, by Monnie Anderson, the author lists 7 suggestions for the visit with an AIDS patient.[28]

1. Prepare for your visit. Pray for God's divine presence of healing, forgiving, sustaining, and redeeming as you visit. Sensitize yourself to God's guidance as you minister to the patient. Call ahead if possible to confirm a good time for the visit. If you make an appointment with the patient make sure to keep it. Nothing is more disappointing to the AIDS patient than when someone who has promised to come does not show. They feel let down once again by God and the church.

2. Knock on the door and show respect for the privacy of the patient. AIDS patients have had all their dignity stripped away, and this helps to restore dignity and exercise control over their situation. Ask if it is a good time to visit, respecting the patient's feelings, privacy and time. Identify yourself and

---

[28] Anderson, Monnie. **Ideas for Hospital Ministries**, 1992. New Hope, Birmingham.

the organization you represent if the patient isn't from your church or doesn't know you. Ask the patient how he/she is doing, not how he/she is feeling, that is the concern of the medical staff. The pastor is concerned with how the patient is doing.

3. Attend to the needs of the patient. If it seems appropriate, pull up a chair and sit close to the patient. This indicates to the patient that you are sincere in your interest in the patient. Ask questions that elicit the feelings of the patient. When you don't know what to say next, make an observation about something in the room. For example, comment on flowers or cards from family and friends if any are visible. Ask about family and friends. Try to discern what is going on inside the patient.

4. Build the trust of the AIDS patient. In the hospital setting, the time required to build trust can be very short. The only way to build trust is to be yourself, be open and accepting, and be trustworthy.

5. Focus on the feelings of the AIDS patient. As we sit and listen to another's story out of love and concern for them, we can recognize their true feelings that sometimes need healing.

6. Offer your emotional support to the AIDS patient. The pastor cannot rescue the patient or fix the problem. But the pastor can be there for the person and offer emotional and spiritual support. The pastor will experience a sense of helplessness by being with the patient. The pastor will also have personal pain as he "weeps with those who weep." It can be very hard and draining on a pastor who ministers to the sick and dying.

7. Offer spiritual support to the AIDS patient. The primary purpose is not to convert the patient, but to minister through God's love. In visiting patients with AIDS we witness to the presence of God who indwells us.

No one has survived AIDS. The patient may live for years with AIDS, but the truth of the matter is it is a terminal disease and the patient **will** die. When the patient dies the pastor must let go. It hurts to lose someone you have become close to. Grief is about saying goodbye and letting go. Grief reduces the pain of loss. In his book *I Don't Know What to Say,* Robert Buckman tells about the stages of grief.

The initial stage of grief often seems like shock. Words which describe the feeling you have at the death of someone close are *in a daze, numb, shocked,* and *just blank.* During this period immediately following the death of the patient, the pastor may be immersed in helping the family or friends with preparations for the funeral or memorial service. After the immediate needs are cared for, a deep sadness follows. You may find yourself emotional. It's OK to cry. Crying helps acknowledge the depth of the hurt. During this stage of grief, you may have physical symptoms of anxiety and distress. The symptoms are normal.

The middle stage of grief usually comes quickly for someone who has been ministering to an AIDS patient because you have lived with the knowledge of impending death throughout the illness. During this stage, life begins to take on some sense of normality. The shock and numbness fade away and you realize that life will go on. Depending on your level of involvement with the patient, you may feel the hardest adjustment being the amount of free time you have after spending many, many hours with the patient.

The resolution stage of grief comes when you are able to look back on your time with the AIDS patient and remember with fondness and pleasure the time you shared. It is during this time that you will be able to identify and articulate truths about life that you learned from this person whose suffering you shared for a time. There is no timetable associated with the resolution stage of grief.

Ministry to the sick and dying is an important part of the pastor's role as shepherd. The pastor will eventually minister to someone in the end-stage of life. This could be from any illness, but it will happen. It is important that the pastor knows ahead of time that it will be an emotionally draining time.

I was in ministry at a church where one of the older members was diagnosed with terminal cancer. The senior pastor asked me take on the ministry to this wonderful lady. The more I visited and got to know her, the closer we became. I learned some valuable lessons during that time. The senior pastor knew what he was doing in assigning me to this woman. She taught me how to do this ministry. It was a tremendous loss to our church and to me personally when she passed away. Ministering to someone in the end-stage of life is a very personal thing and you will become emotionally attached to the person you are ministering to. Just be aware so that you will handle the loss when it comes.

CHAPTER ELEVEN

CANCER

"Cancer is a group of diseases characterized by uncontrolled growth and spread of abnormal cells. If the spread is not controlled, it can result in death. Cancer is caused by both external factors (tobacco, chemicals, radiation, and infectious organisms) and internal factors (inherited mutations, hormones, immune conditions, and mutations that occur from metabolism). Casual factors may act together or in sequence to initiate or promote carcinogenesis. Ten or more years often pass between exposures or mutations and detectable cancer. Cancer is treated by surgery, radiation, chemotherapy, hormones, and immunotherapy."[29]

All parts of the body are made up of cells that divide normally to produce more cells when the body needs them. When cancer occurs, cells keep dividing even when new cells are not needed. The chance from normal to cancerous cells requires several separate, different gene alterations. Eventually, altered genes and uncontrolled growth may produce a tumor that can be benign (not cancer) or malignant

[29] Cancer Facts and Figures 2002. American Cancer Society.

(cancer). Malignant tumors can invade, damage and destroy nearby tissue and spread to other parts of the body. A benign tumor won't spread to other parts of the body but it may damage tissue and need to be removed.

Cancer cells in a malignant tumor may break off and enter the bloodstream or lymphatic system. This is how cancer spreads throughout the body. When cancer spreads to other parts of the body it is said to metastasize. Cancer that spreads to other parts of the body is the same cancer as the original cancer even though it is found elsewhere. [30]

Cancer caused by tobacco and alcohol abuse can be prevented. The American Cancer Society estimates that in 2002, about 170,000 deaths will be caused by tobacco use and 19,000 by alcohol use. There are also an estimated 555,500 deaths expected in relation to nutrition, obesity, and other lifestyles that could also be prevented. Some cancers could be prevented through behavioral changes.

---

[30] National Alliance of Breast Cancer Organizations.

About 1,284,900 new cancer cases are expected to be diagnosed in 2002. Since 1990. about 16 million new cancer cases have been diagnosed. This year about 555,500 Americans are expected to die of cancer, more than 1,500 people a day. Cancer is the second leading cause of death on the U.S. exceeded only by heart disease. In the U.S. I of every 4 deaths is from cancer.[31]

Skin Cancer

Cancer of the skin is the most common of all cancers. Melanoma accounts for about 4% of skin cancer cases, but it causes about 79% of skin cancer deaths. The number of new cases of melanoma in the United States is on the rise. The American Cancer Society estimates that in 2002 there will be 53,600 new cases of melanoma in the country and about 7,400 will die from this disease.

Melanoma is the most serious form of skin cancer. If diagnosed and removed while it is still thin and limited to the outermost skin layer, it is almost 100% curable. Once the cancer metastasizes

[31] Cancer Facts and Figures 2002. American Cancer Socitety.

(spreads) to other parts of the body, it is hard to treat and can be deadly.

Melanoma is a malignant tumor that originates in melanocytes, the cells which produce the pigment melanin that colors our skin, hair, eyes and is most heavily concentrated in moles. The majority of melanomas are black or brown. Melanomas occasionally stop producing pigment. When that happens, the melanomas may no longer be dark, but are skin-colored, pink, red, or purple.

A doctor can determine whether the melanoma is in the early stage or advanced. Melanoma that has not advanced is usually referred to as *in situ* which is Latin for "in one site" or "localized." These melanomas occupy only the uppermost part of the epidermis, the top layers of the skin. Invasive melanomas are the more serious because they have gone more deeply into the skin and may have traveled through the body.[32]

---

[32] *About Melanoma.* The Skin Cancer Foundation.

Basal Cell carcinoma is the most common form of skin cancer. Basal cell carcinoma affects 800,000 Americans each year. It is the most common of all cancers. One out of every three new cancers is a skin cancer. These cancers arise in the basal cells, which are at the bottom of the epidermis (outer skin layer).

Chronic exposure to sunlight is the cause of almost all basal cell carcinomas, which occur most frequently on exposed parts of the body-the face, ears, neck, scalp, shoulders, and back. Anyone with a history of frequent exposure to the sun can develop basal cell carcinoma.

Squamous cell carcinoma is the second most common skin cancer. It afflicts more than 200,000 Americans each year. It arises from the epidermis and resembles squamous cells that comprise most of the upper layers of skin. Squamous cell cancers may occur on all areas of the body including the mucous membranes, but are most common in areas exposed to the sun.[33]

---

[33] *About Squamous Cell.* The Skin Cancer Foundation.

Lung Cancer

Lung cancer is the second most common cancer among both men and women and is the leading cause of cancer death in both sexes. Cigarette smoking accounts for nearly 90% of all lung cancers. Passive smoking also contributes to the development of lung cancer among nonsmokers. Certain occupational exposures such as asbestos exposure are also known to cause lung cancer.[34]

Lung cancer comes from abnormal cells that are growing out-of-control. Lung cancer begins in the lungs. The lungs are two sponge-like organs found in the chest. The right lung has three sections, called lobes. The left lung has two lobes. The left lung is smaller because the heart is also on that side. The lining around the lungs, called the pleura, helps to protect the lungs and allows them to move during breathing. The windpipe (trachea) brings air down into the lungs. It divides into tubes called bronchi, which divide into smaller

---

[34] *Lung and Bronchus-U.S. Racial/Ethnic Cancer Patterns.* National Cancer Institute.

branches called bronchioles. At the end of these small branches are tiny air sacs know as alveoli.[35]

Most lung cancers start in the lining of the bronchi, but they can start in other parts of the lung. It often takes many years for lung cancer to develop. Once the cancer develops and begins to grow, cells break away and spread to other parts of the body in a process known as metastasis. Lung cancer is a life-threatening disease. It often spreads to other parts of the body before it is found.

Lung cancer is the leading cancer killer in both men and women. There were an estimated 164,100 new cases of lung cancer and an estimated 156,900 deaths from lung cancer in the United States in 2000.[36]

Smoking is the number one cause of lung cancer. Eighty-seven percent of lung cancer cases are caused by smoking and could probably have been prevented. Cigarette smoke contains more than

---

[35] *What is Lung Cancer?* American Cancer Society.
[36] *Facts About Lung Cancer.* American Lung Association.

4000 different chemicals, many of which are proven cancer-causing substances, or carcinogens.

Many of the chemicals in tobacco smoke also affect the nonsmoker inhaling the smoke, making "secondhand smoking" another important cause of lung cancer. It is responsible for approximately 3000 lung cancer deaths and as many as 62,000 deaths from heart disease annually.[37]

Radon is considered to be the second leading cause of lung cancer in the U.S. today. Radon causes between 15,999-20,000 lung cancer deaths each year in the United States.

Another leading cause of lung cancer is on-the-job exposure to carcinogens. Asbestos is a well-known work-related substance that can cause lung cancer.

---

[37] ibid

Breast Cancer

Breast cancer is the most common form of cancer in women in the United States, other than skin cancer. It is the second leading cause of cancer death in women, after lung cancer. About 203,500 women in the United States will be diagnosed with invasive breast cancer in 2002. And about 40,000 women will die from the disease in 2002.[38]

In the United States, one out of nine women will develop breast cancer during her lifetime. The risk of developing breast cancer increases with age. The risk also increases for women with a family history of breast cancer. However, 70% of breast cancer cases occur in women who have no identifiable risk factors.

Colorectal Cancer

The American Cancer Society estimates that there will be 107,300 new cases of colon cancer and 41,000 new cases of rectal cancer in 2002 in the United States. Colon cancer will cause about 48,100

---

[38] *How Many Women get Breast Cancer?* American Cancer Society.

deaths and rectal cancer about 8,500 deaths in the United States in 2002. The death rate from colorectal cancer has been going down for the past 20 years. This may be due to better nutrition, early detection, or improved treatments.[39]

Remember that cancer is caused by abnormal cells that grow out-of-control. Colorectal cancer begins in either the colon or the rectum when some of these abnormal cells begin growing out-of-control. The colon and the rectum are both part of the digestive tract, also called the GI (gastrointestinal) tract.

To better understand colon cancer let's take a look at the digestive system. The GI tract is where food is processed to create energy and rid the body of waste. After food is chewed and swallowed, it travels down the esophagus to the stomach. There it is partly broken down and sent to the small intestine. The small intestine continues breaking down the food and absorbs most of the nutrients. The small intestine is the longest section of the GI tract. It joins the large intestine (large

---

[39] *What is Colorectal Cancer?* American Cancer Society.

bowel), a muscular tube about five feet long. The first part of the large bowel, called the colon, continues to absorb water and nutrients from the food and also serves as a storage place for waste matter. The waste matter moves from the colon into the rectum. From there it passes out of the body. The colon has four sections: the ascending colon, the transverse colon, the descending colon, and the sigmoid colon. Cancer can start in any of the four sections or in the rectum. Each of these sections of the colon and rectum has several layers of tissue. Cancer starts in the innermost layer and can grow through some or all of the other layers. Knowing a little about the layers is helpful because the stage (extent of the spread) of colorectal cancer depends on the layers affected. It can begin in any part of the colon or rectum.. Colorectal cancers probably develop slowly over a period of several years. There are often early signs. One sign is a change in growth of tissue called a polyp. Removing the polyp early may prevent it from becoming cancer.[40]

---

[40] *What is Colorectal Cancer?* American Cancer Society.

Cancer Facts

Everyone is at risk of cancer developing cancer. The occurrence of cancer increases as individuals age and affects most adults beginning in middle age. About 77% of all cancers are diagnosed at ages 55 and older. Lifetime risk refers to the probability that an individual, over the course of a lifetime, will develop cancer or die from it. In the US, men have a little less than 1 in 2 lifetime risk of developing cancer; for women the risk is a little more than 1 in 3. Relative risk is a measure of the strength of the relationship between risk factors and the particular cancer. It compares the risk of developing cancer in persons with certain exposure or trait to the risk in persons who do not have the exposure or trait.

All cancers involve the malfunction of genes that control cell growth and division. About 5% to 10% of cancers are clearly hereditary, in that an inherited faulty gene predisposes the person to a very high risk of particular cancers. The remainder of cancers are not hereditary, but result from damage to genes (mutations) that occur throughout the lifetime.[41]

Facts and Figures

- NCI estimates 8.9 million Americans with a history of cancer were alive in 1997.
- About 1,284,900 new cases are expected to be diagnosed in 2002.
- Since 1990, about 16 million new cancer cases have been diagnosed.
- In 2002, about 555,500 Americans are expected to die of cancer.
- Cancer is the second leading cause of death in the US.
- In the US, 1 of every 4 deaths is from cancer.
- The 5-year relative survival rate for all cancers combined is 62%[42]

---

[41] American Cancer Society, "Cancer Facts and Figures 2002."

[42] American Cancer Society, "Cancer Facts and Figures 2002."

I have included this information to better equip the pastor in caring for the cancer patient. Cancer is a widespread disease that touches all ethnic groups and both genders. It will strike in the church community. I hope that the information provided here has given the pastoral care provider a little more understanding of the disease. I would suggest that if you are providing care for a cancer patient that you become knowledgeable in that particular cancer. It will help you to better understand what the patient is going through and help in your ministering to him/her.

CHAPTER TWELVE

FINAL DECISIONS

Advance Directives

Most states have legal documents that speak for the patient when the patient is unable to speak for himself/herself. These documents are written while the patient is still of sound mind and able to express the desire. The living will and healthcare proxy are legal documents that are administered according to state law. The do-not-resuscitate order is a medical directive filed with the doctor and hospital. The patient should discuss these documents with the family and doctor so they understand the patient's wishes.

Living Will

This document may have a different name in differing states, but it is a document that outlines the types of treatment the patient would or would not like in the event they have been given a terminal diagnosis, that death is imminent and unavoidable, or the patient is in a terminally persistent vegetative state. Most states have a requirement of 2 or more doctors recording the diagnosis as terminal. This document aids the doctor in determining which treatment to administer when the patient cannot speak for himself/herself.

Healthcare Proxy

This document is also called a Durable Medical Power of Attorney. This document provides the name of the person or persons who will make decisions about the patient's healthcare when the patient is unable to make the decisions himself/herself. This document does not require that you be in a terminal state. The proxy will have the power and the authority to make health care decisions on behalf of the patient when it is determined that the patient is incapable of making an informed decision about providing, withholding, or withdrawing medical treatment. This document can also include the intentions of the grantor. For example, the grantor can state that if in a permanent vegetative state the grantor does not want to be kept alive by medical intervention but would like actions appropriate to keep in reasonable comfort and cleanliness. The grantor may state that he/she would like measures taken to keep him/her comfortable, hydrated, given pain medication, but be allowed to die.

Do-Not-Resuscitate Order

The Do-Not-Resuscitate (DNR) Order is a medical order to refrain from cardiopulmonary resuscitation if a patient's heart stops beating. When a patient's heart stops beating or breathing stops, medical workers always attempt cardiopulmonary resuscitation to revive the patient. Often those with terminal illnesses or those in the final stages of cancer may choose to forego CPR. The doctor and patient may discuss this and decide on a DNR Order. The staff will be made aware of the order; it will be filed in the patient's chart and may be posted on the patient's door. In the event the patient's heart stops or breathing stops, CPR and other measures to resuscitate will not be taken.

The following is a paper I did as a project in my CPE class. I believe that patients should not only be given the opportunity to sign a DNR upon admission to a healthcare facility, but should also be given the opportunity to sign an Allow Natural Death (AND) Order. This is a positive approach to death.

ALLOW NATURAL DEATH

"Precious in the sight of the Lord is the death of his saints." (Psalm 116:15) Society today views death as something to be prolonged, put off until sometime in the future. Extreme measures are taken to preserve life even if it is evident that the attempts are futile. At what point should we say, "Pull the plug, stop the feeding, allow the patient to die?" It is my belief that everyone has the right to die a natural death without extensive intervention to prolong life.

"All the days ordained for me were written in your book before one of them came to be." (Psalm 139:16) God has given each of us a certain number of days to live on earth, and has recorded those days in Heaven. I believe that if it is our time to die, if we have completed our appointed number of days, then we have the right to pass from earth to heaven, to pass from life on earth to life in heaven. I believe that the saved only go through death of the body, and that the soul instantly passes into the immediate presence of our Lord. I believe

that to prolong the death of the body keeps the soul from the appointed time to enter into the Lord's presence.

"And even the very hairs of your head are all numbered." (Matthew 10:30) Our Father knows everything about us. He knows what afflicts our bodies. God does not cause our infirmities. He is aware of everything that happens to us. He knows when we are in pain and suffering. The good news is that He is with us throughout all of our trials. We are the firstfruits of His creation and He loves us.

"Just as man is destined to die once, and after that to face judgment."(Hebrews 9:27) Each of us is appointed a time to die. We are to physically die once. The question arises, should attempts be made to revive or resuscitate a person who has died? CPR is used when a person's heart and/or breathing has stopped. Many lives are saved each year by reviving a person using CPR. Is that going against God's will? What if the heart stops due to an accident, would it go against God's will to revive that person? Is that a natural death? Is that in God's timing?

In the hospital setting, if a patient's heart stops or if the patient ceases breathing an attempt is automatically made to revive the patient unless an order is previously made to the contrary. Upon admission, the patient is generally given the opportunity to sign a "Do Not Resuscitate" order (DNR). This decision is then noted on the patient's chart and the staff is made aware of the decision. It is my belief that rather than only offering a DNR to the patient, the patient should also be given the opportunity to sign an "Allow Natural Death" order (AND). By giving the option of an AND order, the patient is given the right to die a natural death with dignity. If the patient has taken this positive approach to death he/she would be allowed to die without the efforts of CPR, artificial nourishment or hydration, ventilation, or any other life-sustaining attempts.

Many patients have benefited from artificial feeding and hydration. Feeding tubes are used when a patient can no longer take food or liquids by mouth. Feeding tubes can be long or short term. The nasogastric tube is inserted through the nose, down the esophagus and into the stomach. The gastrostomy is a tube inserted surgically through the skin into the stomach wall. Water and liquid nutritional supplements can be poured into the tube or pumped in using a mechanical device [43](Dunn).

For the purpose of this discussion, the IV tube used to administer medications and fluids short-term to patients who are not dying is excluded. The use of an IV to hydrate a dying patient is, in my opinion, neither palliative nor life-extending. I believe that a dying patient should be allowed to make the decision to allow a natural death by refusing artificial nutrition and hydration. The thought of withdrawing artificial nutrition and hydration from a patient becomes a moral and ethical issue. It is a decision that can cause great anguish for families. Studies have shown that death after the withdrawal of artificial nutrition and hydration will usually be comfortable. Continued treatment may cause considerable discomfort from fluid overload. Seriously ill or dying patients experience little if any discomfort upon the withdrawal of tube feedings or intravenous hydration because of the release of opiods or the analgesic effects of ketosis. In one series of studies, terminally ill patients who preferred to refuse nutrition but felt obligated to eat to please their families

[43] "Hard Choices for Loving People," Hank Dunn.

suffered abdominal discomfort and nausea. Case reports illustrate a high level of comfort and satisfaction among patients that may accompany dying after refusing nutrition and hydration. [44](NEJM 2/27/97)

I am convinced that to force food and water on a dying patient is both morally and ethically wrong. It can cause the patient to experience undue comfort and may lead to complications such as infections and pneumonia. If food and water are withheld, the patient will probably die from dehydration and not starvation. There are benefits of dehydration in the dying patient. Dehydration causes less fluids in the lungs and therefore less congestion, making breathing easier. Dehydration also causes less fluid in the throat, therefore there is less need for suctioning. There is less pressure around tumors causing less pain. Dehydration causes less urination and less need for changing the bed and less risk of bedsores. In dehydration, there is a natural release of pain-relieving chemicals as the body dehydrates.

---

[44] "Withdrawing Intensive Life-Sustaining Treatment-Recommendations for Compassionate Clinical Management," Howard Brody, et al. **New England Journal of Medicine**, February 27, 1997, Vol. 336, No. 9.

[45](Dunn) A person who is in the dying process cannot properly digest food. Body systems and organs begin to fail. Forcing a patient to eat may cause discomfort and pain. I believe that when a patient is dying, he/she has the right to refuse nutrition and hydration. Patients can be kept comfortable by giving them small sips of water, ice chips, or by swabbing the mouth. Vaseline can be used to keep the lips moist. These things can be done to give the patient comfort, while allowing them to die a natural death without using life-sustaining nutrition or hydration. If a patient had an AND order it would take the pressure off the family to make decisions about prolonging the life and thus possibly causing the patient more pain.

When I reflect upon the dying process of my grandmother, I find comfort in the way we allowed her to die a natural death. She had multiple myeloma and died seven months after her diagnosis. She was in her nineties and remained very active until she became ill with this cancer. The doctors convinced her to try chemo and radiation therapy. She was only able to withstand one treatment of each. My grandmother was a strong woman and devout Christian. She lived a

---

[45] "Hard Choices for Loving People," Hank Dunn.

long, productive life and was ready to go home to the Lord. We talked at great length about her wish to die naturally, with dignity. I went back to be with her on weekends until her last two months when my mom, aunt and I stayed with her until the end. I learned a lot about dying during those two months.

When we have Jesus in our life, He is there to stay. He doesn't leave when the going gets tough; he picks us up and carries us. Jesus was in my grandma's room caring for all of us. She had made the decision to die naturally. She had chosen not to be revived, not to have a feeding tube, not to have any life-sustaining procedures done. Her last week was the hardest for the family. She had stopped eating. Family members encouraged her to take nourishment. When grandma tried to drink the Ensure offered to her, she would choke or begin vomiting. Her body was ready to die. God was calling her home. She was ready to go. Jesus was in the room holding my grandma in His arms. I talked with my grandma and told her that I respected her wishes to not eat and that it was ok to go home to the Lord. For the last two days of my grandma's life, family members sat at her bedside swabbing her mouth and moistening her lips to keep her comfortable.

She passed away in the still of the night. Her physical body was left behind but her soul passed into the immediate presence of our Lord. What right do we have to delay the dying process? What right do we have to keep a person from joining their Lord at the moment He calls him/her? I believe that a person has the right to pass from this life into eternity in God's time.

I am convinced that the medical profession needs to review the policies and procedures concerning death and dying, and initiate a positive approach. Upon admission to a hospital, patients could be offered an AND which would allow them to die a natural death. It could be a legal document that would absolve the hospital of liability if the patient dies. This would be a new approach. The DNR and other such orders take the negative approach. They state what attempts are not to be taken. An AND would allow the patient to die naturally with no life-prolonging attempts. The AND is a positive approach to death of the body.

God has appointed all to die once. To perform CPR or any other such life-sustaining actions on me would be going against God's will.

I look forward to the time when I leave my earthly body and join my Savior. I know that I have things to accomplish on earth. When I have completed what God has intended for me to do; I will be called home. I do not believe anyone has the right to take that away from me. Many argue that accidents happen and that it really isn't our time. I believe that God is in control and if we aren't to die, we won't. In cases where death is not eminent, then medical intervention is warranted. I just do not believe that if a person is dying, man has the right to stop that process.

During the dying process, I believe the emphasis should be on pain management and quality of life. Letting a person die naturally does not mean that we stop caring for him/her. Our care is just shifted from the focus of cure to comfort. Patients should continue to receive pain medication. The time a patient has left can be spent on things that are important to them. Many find that during the dying process they become closer to their Lord. It can be a time of confession and cleansing of the soul. It can be a time where the patient reminisces and enjoys talking about times past. By allowing the patient to die naturally, without prolonging the process, we allow the patient to pass with dignity.

As a Christian, I long for the day when I can go home to the Lord. I do not want extensive medical treatments. I do not want to be brought back if I have died. I have seen patients who have diseases, which are ravaging their bodies. If the patient is terminal then attempts to cure the illness may be futile. Not only is the treatment of the disease keeping the patient from enjoying what time he/she has left it is also costly. I do not want any efforts in futility extended on my behalf. I want to die with dignity. I have the right to be allowed to die a natural death. I believe that all have the right to a natural death. It is God's will that when our days are fulfilled, our physical body dies and our souls go to Him.

I believe that my convictions in this area are in alignment with the Baptist tradition. Baptists believe in the sanctity of life. We also believe that only God knows when our time on earth is up. If we are called home to be with the Lord, then man must not interfere with God's timing. I believe that when a person is clearly terminal and attempts to keep the person alive will be futile, then that person should be kept comfortable and allowed to die a natural death, if that is the person's wish.

Baptists are born again and know that upon death they will be in the immediate presence of the Lord. To deny a born again Christian the right to go home to the Lord is incomprehensible to me. Some of the efforts made by the medical world are outside the ethics that Baptists believe.

My opinions and beliefs in this area have been formed through reading, personal reflection, conversations with other pastors, and through interaction with patients. I have spent much time in prayer and reflection. I have watched patients grasp for anything that may extend their life. I have seen patients who have accepted that their condition will never improve. The extent to which a patient is treated should be up to the patient. I am convinced that the approach to death should be positive by allowing patients to die a natural death, if it is the patient's wish.

HOSPICE

Hospice is a concept of caring that provides comfort and support for those who are terminally ill with a life expectation of six months or less.[46] Hospice refers to the steadily growing concept of humane and compassionate care, which can be implemented in a variety of settings-in patient's homes, in hospitals, or in freestanding inpatient facilities. Hospice provides a team of professionals and trained volunteers to address medical, social, psychological, and spiritual needs of patients and their families. The emphasis of Hospice is on management of pain and other symptoms and quality of life rather than on cure and length of life.[47]

Hospice allows the patient and family to focus on life and make the most out of the time left. Hospice neither hastens death nor prolongs life. The purpose of Hospice is to control pain and discomfort. This affords the patient dignity. The family plays an

---

[46] On Our Own Terms, Moyers on Dying. *What is Hospice? By Jack Gordon.*
[47] Hard Choices for Loving People, Frank Dunn.

active role in determining the care plan for the patient with the help of the hospice care team.

Hospice allows for the patient's care in the home. Most would like to spend their final days in their home, surrounded by family and a familiar environment. More than 80% of Hospice care in the U.S. takes place in the home.[48] Some Hospice care takes place in a free standing Hospice Care facility.

Comfort Measures

Some measures are clearly meant to bring comfort to the patient but not prolong the life or the dying process. Pain medication helps to reduce the pain but will not prolong the dying process. Keeping the patient clean will give comfort to the patient. Hospice also provides care for the patient's emotional and spiritual well-being. The focus of Hospice is comfort.

---

[48] On Our Own Terms, Moyer on Dying. *What is Hospice? By Jack Gordon.*

In the Hospice approach new treatments may be withheld. Cancer patients who receive chemo and radiation treatments may no longer receive them under Hospice, unless they are used to relieve pain. Antibiotics may not be used to treat infection, but may be used to relieve pain. Diagnostic testing would be eliminated especially any procedure that might be painful to the patient. Feeding tubes would not be started and may be removed. Surgery would not be performed unless to promote the comfort of the patient.[49]

Patients and families who turn to Hospice or comfort care near the end of life are allowing time for the celebration of life. During this time the family and patient can reconcile any differences and heal broken relationships. The patient can reflect on his/her life and share joyful memories with others. The time also allows for good-byes and for healing to take place.

Palliative Care

Palliative, or "comfort" care recognizes that death is a normal part of life and tries to prepare patients and families to meet it so that we

---

[49] Hard Choices for Dying People, Frank Dunn.

can all die on our own terms. Palliative care takes place in the hospital, extended care facility, or nursing home instead of in the home like Hospice. Palliative care teams are made up of doctors, nurses and other professional medical caregivers at a medical care facility. They administer the patient's on-going comfort-care.

Patients can receive palliative care at any time. They do not need to be within six months of death to be eligible as in Hospice.

Palliative care services include: [50]

- Curative or life-prolonging treatments. Palliative care patients can receive all of the benefits of comfort care while continuing curative treatment for their condition.
- Relief of physical suffering. Palliative care professionals provide highly skilled symptom management for pain, anxiety, constipation, weakness, and many other kinds of discomfort.

[50] On Our Own Terms, Bill Moyers. *What is Palliative Care? Dr. Diane Meier.*

They also help patients and families deal with side effects of therapies.

- Attention to emotional needs. Palliative care recognizes that emotional and spiritual distresses are important sources of suffering. Palliative care teams can offer help with non-physical pain through counseling and spiritual support.

- Communication. Palliative care teams are made up not only of medical and nursing practitioners, but social workers, clergy, pharmacists, and physical and occupational therapists. These teams work together to determine the needs of the patient.

- Support for the bereaved family. Palliative care programs recognize that family caregivers need help and support after an illness and make support and counseling services available to them.

Funeral/Memorial Service Information

The pastor will need to meet with the family and perhaps the patient to discuss the funeral or memorial service. A patient who has a terminal illness will probably want to be involved in making these decisions or at least be included in the decision-making. Sudden deaths do not allow for the pastor to meet with the person to plan the funeral. This can be a very difficult time for families so great care and compassion must be afforded the family.

It is a good idea to develop your own form to carry with you to the meeting. A form prepared ahead of time will help you to remember all the information that you need to gather. At the very least, take good notes.

A sample information form follows on the next page.

Funeral/Memorial Service Information Form

Full Name: ________________________ Maiden Name: __________
Address: ____________________________________
____
____

I would prefer (please check the appropriate spaces):
____ Memorial Service, burial preceding
____ Funeral, burial following
____ Memorial Service, cremation preceding
____ Funeral, cremation following
____ Interment to be public
____ Interment to be private
____ Casket closed
____ Casket open prior to service
____ Casket open during service
____ Casket open following service

Other instructions or requests:

If cremation is chosen, what would you like done with the ashes?

Where would you like for the funeral/memorial service to be held?

Funeral/Memorial Service Requests:

1. Favorite Hymns:
2. Is there a specific soloist you would like to sing?
3. Favorite Scriptures:
4. Favorite Poetry (attach a copy):
5. Personal Words to leave (brief testimony):
6. Who would you like to conduct the service?
7. If more than one minister, what part would you like each to have?
8. Are there any others that you would like to participate?

Many loved ones and friends prefer the custom of giving memorial contributions to a church, a mission organization, school, or charity, in lieu of flowers. Please express your wishes.

Burial:

Are you a member of a Memorial/Burial Association? (Please specify name and address)

Do you have burial insurance, a pre-arranged and/or pre-paid arrangement? With whom?

Are you eligible for veterans or military funeral and flag?

Do you have a cemetery plot? If so, where?

Do you have a will? Who has copies?

Have you donated any part of your body to science?

Loss, Grief, and Bereavement

Anticipatory Grief

Anticipatory grief is similar to the normal process of mourning, but it occurs before the actual death. Anticipatory grief occurs before death, often as a result of a terminal diagnosis or to a life-threatening illness, when death is a possibility. Anticipatory grief can be experienced by: family, loved ones, and the dying. Everyone experiences grief in their own way, but there are some common stages.

Grief may include the following phases, possibly in multiple times, intensities, and orders. The following are extracted from *"Care of the Terminally Ill Child"* by the University of Utah Health Sciences Center.

- Phase I: The individual realizes that death is inevitable and there is no expectation of a cure. Sadness and depression often occur in the first stage of grief.

- Phase II: This phase is the concern for the dying. Family members may regret arguments with the dying. For the dying, concern may be increased for themselves and their fear of death.
- Phase III: The actual death may be "rehearsed." Funeral arrangements and saying good-bye to loved ones may occur in this phase of anticipatory grief.
- Phase IV: Loved ones may imagine what their lives are going to be like without the person who is dying. The person dying may think about life after death. The dying may also think about what it will be like for his/her loved ones without him/her.[51]

Others have identified emotional paths of the grieving as follows:

John Bowlby, <u>Attachment and Loss: Vol. III,</u> 4 Phases

1. Numbing
2. Yearning and searching for the lost figure
3. Disorganization and despair

4. Reorganization

Glen W. Davidson, Understanding Mourning, A Guide For Those Who Grieve, 4 Phases

1. Shock and numbness
2. Searching and Yearning
3. Disorientation
4. Reorganization

Richard A Dershimer, Counseling the Bereaved, 4 Phases

1. Shock
2. Acute Grief
3. Straightening up the mess
4. Reinvesting and reengaging in life

Elizabeth Kubler-Ross, On Death and Dying, 5 Stages

1. Denial
2. Anger

---

[51] University of Utah Health Sciences Center. *Care of the Terminally Ill Child.*2001.

3. Bargaining
4. Depression
5. Acceptance

Collin Murray-Parkes, Recovery from Bereavement, 3 Tasks

1. Intellectual acceptance of the loss
2. Emotional acceptance of the loss
3. A change in the individual's model of self and outer world to match the new reality

Therese Rando, Treatment of Complicated Mourning, 3 Phases/ 6 Processes

Avoidance phase:

1. Recognize the loss

Confrontation phase:

2. React to the separation
3. Recollect and re-experience the deceased and the relationship
4. Relinquish the old attachments to the deceased and the old assumptive world

Accomodation phase:

5. Readjust to move more adaptively into the new world without forgetting the old
6. Reinvest meaningfully in life

John Schneider, The Transformative Power of Grief, 3 levels

1. Discovering what is lost
2. Discovering what is left
3. Finding what is possible as a consequence

J. William Worden, Grief Counseling and Grief Therapy, 4 Tasks

1. Acceptance of the reality of the loss
2. Experiencing the pain of grief
3. Adjustment to an environment in which the deceased is missing
4. Emotionally relocating the deceased and moving on with life

Bereavement is the state of having suffered a loss and experiencing many emotions and changes. There is no set amount of time a person spends in this state. Grief is the process of reacting to the loss. The reaction to a physical loss is determined by many factors, such as the relationship to the person who has died, or if that death was anticipated. Grief can be expressed as a mental, physical or emotional reaction. Mental reactions can include anger, guilt, anxiety, sadness, and despair. Physical reactions can include sleeping problems, changes in appetite, or illness. Social reactions can include the taking care of other family members, seeing family members, or the return to work. Grief may be described as the presence of physical problems, constant thoughts of the person who died, guilt, hostility, and a change in the way a person normally acts.[52]

Mourning is the conscious, unconscious, and cultural reactions to loss. Mourning is the process of how one incorporates the experienced loss into their ongoing life. Those who are grieving spend a lot of physical and emotional energy and can become very tired. Those in mourning not only grieve the loss of the person, but also the loss of unfulfilled dreams. There are three stages to mourning: the urge to

[52] University of Pennsylvania Cancer Center, NCI/PDQ Patient Information: Loss, grief, and bereavement. June 2000.

bring back the person who died, disorganization and sadness, and reorganization.

The mourner must go through a process of separating himself/herself from the person who died. The mourner must find a new way to direct the energy that was formerly directed to the one who died. The person's role and identity may be changed.

CHAPTER THIRTEEN

ETHICS

Information regarding clinical ethics is given to help the pastor understand the ethics involved in research and treatments using experimental treatment plans and medicine. It is good for the pastor to know a bit about the ethics involved if one of his flock wants to discuss proposed procedures or treatments. This is not meant to be exhaustive, but rather an overview of terms and codification. This information was taken from material provided to CPE students at the National Institutes of Health in Bethesda, Maryland.

Ethics is a branch of philosophy. It is a way of thinking about morality (one's sense of obligations), moral problems and moral judgments. Clinical ethics can be defined as that branch of ethics that

- Concentrates on issues as they arise in clinical practice or clinical research.

- Includes the identification, analysis and resolution of moral problems (values conflicts) that arise in the care of a particular patient or subject or in the design or implementation of a clinical protocol.

- Is distinguished by the fact that it must focus on practical decisions.

A moral dilemma can be defined as a real situation in which:

- Knowledge of what is good or right is confused, contradictory or absent.

- The justification of choice of one option over the other is not convincing.

Ethical principles include:

- Respect for Autonomy: Respecting each person's values, perspectives and capacities and enabling others to act autonomously.

- Nonmaleficence: doing no harm, preventing harm.

- Beneficence: Doing and/or promoting good.

- Justice: Treating equals equally and unequals, unequally. Fair distribution of benefits and burdens.

Traditional Ethical Theories:

- Consequentialist Theories: Maximizing the good, the greatest good for the greatest number, consequences are what count the most.

- Deontologic Theories: What do our Codes of Ethics say? What counts the most are meeting our duties and obligations.

- Virtue Ethics: Consequences and duties and obligations are important, but what is the most important is that we act out of virtuous motives.

Traditional Perspectives through which Values are Filtered:

- Consequentialism: The goodness of an act is determined by its consequences.

- Deontology: The goodness of an act is determined by whether or not the person performing the act met his/her duties and obligations.

- Virtue ethics: The goodness of an act is determined by whether or not the motives of the person performing the act were virtuous.

Contemporary and Additional Approaches to Ethical Analysis:

- Feminist Ethics: Behavior occurs in relation to others. Add considerations of interdependence and relationships. Ethical analysis is incomplete without special attention to contextual concerns such as care, compassion, power and oppression.

- Communitarian Ethics: Behavior occurs within a social environment. Add consideration of social context, social history and the customs and moral norms of specific communities and groups.

Boundaries Between Practice and Research:

- Practice refers to interventions that are designed solely to enhance the well-being of an individual patient or client and that have a reasonable expectation of success.

- The purpose of medical or behavioral practice is to provide diagnosis, preventive intervention or therapy to particular individuals.

Research is defined as a systematic study designed to develop or contribute to generalized knowledge.

Applying Ethical Principles to Research:

Applications of the basic ethical principles to the conduct of research, leads to the consideration of the following requirements:

- Informed consent: Respect for persons requires that subjects, to the degree they are capable, be given the opportunity to choose what shall or shall not happen to them.

- This opportunity is provided when adequate standards for informed consent are satisfied. Agreement exists that the three primary components of informed consent are: information, comprehension, voluntariness.

- Assessments of risks and benefits- Research must show a favorable risk/benefit assessment, that is, the risk, or possibility of harm must be outweighed by the expectation of benefit, or positive value, related to health or welfare.

- Selection of Subjects. There are to be fair procedures and outcomes in the selection of research subjects. Requirements of social justice dictate that distinctions be made between classes of subjects that ought, and ought not, participate in any particular kind of research, based on the ability of members of that class to bear burdens and on the appropriateness of placing further burdens on already burdened persons.

Codification of Research Ethics:

1. The Nuremberg Code, 1947
2. Declaration of Helsinki, World Medical Assembly, Helsinki, Finland, 1964, revised, Tokyo, Japan, 1975.
3. *The Belmont Report*, issued by the National Commission for the Protection of Human Subjects of Biomedical and Behavioral Research, April 18, 1979.

4. *Protection of Human Subjects* - 45 CFR 46: OPRR (Office for the Protection from Research Risks) Reports, National Institutes of Health, Public Health Service, first issued July 12, 1974, revised March 8, 1983 and June 18, 1991.
5. International Ethical Guidelines for Biomedical Research involving Human Subjects: Prepared by the Council for International Organizations of Medical Services (CIOMS) in collaboration with the World Health Organization (WHO).

CHAPTER FOURTEEN

SPIRITUAL READINGS

Spiritual Readings

Psalm 23:1-6

A Psalm of David.

The LORD *is* my shepherd; I shall not want.

2He maketh me to lie down in green pastures: he leadeth me
beside the still waters.

3He restoreth my soul: he leadeth me in the paths of righteousness
for his name's sake.

4Yea, though I walk through the valley of the shadow of death, I
will fear no evil: for thou *art* with me; thy rod and thy staff they
comfort me.

5Thou preparest a table before me in the presence of mine
enemies: thou anointest my head with oil; my cup runneth over.

6Surely goodness and mercy shall follow me all the days of my
life: and I will dwell in the house of the LORD for ever.

The Lord's Prayer

Matthew 6:9-13

After this manner therefore pray ye:

Our Father which art in heaven, Hallowed be thy name.

10Thy kingdom come. Thy will be done in earth, as *it is* in heaven.

11Give us this day our daily bread.

12And forgive us our debts, as we forgive our debtors.

13And lead us not into temptation, but deliver us from evil: For thine is the kingdom, and the power, and the glory, for ever. Amen.

Matthew 10:30

But the very hairs of your head are all numbered.

Psalm 22:24

For he hath not despised nor abhorred the affliction of the afflicted; neither hath he hid his face from him; but when he cried unto him, he heard.

Psalm 34:17-19

The righteous cry, and the LORD heareth, and delivereth them out
of all their troubles. 18The LORD *is* nigh unto them that are of a broken
heart; and saveth such as be of a contrite spirit.

19Many *are* the afflictions of the righteous: but the LORD delivereth him out of them all.

Psalm 46:1-11

To the chief Musician for the sons of Korah, A Song upon Alamoth.

God *is* our refuge and strength, a very present help in trouble.

2Therefore will not we fear, though the earth be removed, and
though the mountains be carried into the midst of the sea;

3*Though* the waters thereof roar *and* be troubled, *though* the
mountains shake with the swelling thereof. Selah.

4*There is* a river, the streams whereof shall make glad the city of
God, the holy *place* of the tabernacles of the most High.

5God *is* in the midst of her; she shall not be moved: God shall help
her, *and that* right early.

6The heathen raged, the kingdoms were moved: he uttered his
voice, the earth melted.

7The LORD of hosts *is* with us; the God of Jacob *is* our refuge.
Selah.

8Come, behold the works of the LORD, what desolations he hath
made in the earth.

9He maketh wars to cease unto the end of the earth; he breaketh the bow, and cutteth the spear in sunder; he burneth the chariot in the fire.

10Be still, and know that I *am* God: I will be exalted among the heathen, I will be exalted in the earth.

11The LORD of hosts *is* with us; the God of Jacob *is* our refuge. Selah.

Psalm 48:14

For this God *is* our God for ever and ever: he will be our guide *even* unto death.

Psalm 55:22

Cast thy burden upon the LORD, and he shall sustain thee: he shall never suffer the righteous to be moved.

Psalm 73:23-25

Nevertheless I *am* continually with thee: thou hast holden *me* by my right hand.

24Thou shalt guide me with thy counsel, and afterward receive me
to glory.

25Whom have I in heaven *but thee?* and *there is* none upon earth
that I desire beside thee.

Psalm 84:11-12

For the LORD God *is* a sun and shield: the LORD will give grace and glory: no good *thing* will he withhold from them that walk uprightly.

12O LORD of hosts, blessed *is* the man that trusteth in thee.

Psalm 91:1-2

He that dwelleth in the secret place of the most High shall abide under the shadow of the Almighty.

2I will say of the LORD, *He is* my refuge and my fortress: my God;
in him will I trust.

Isaiah 40:28-31

Hast thou not known? hast thou not heard, *that* the everlasting God, the LORD, the Creator of the ends of the earth, fainteth not, neither is weary? *there is* no searching of his understanding.

29He giveth power to the faint; and to *them that have* no might he increaseth strength.

30Even the youths shall faint and be weary, and the young men shall utterly fall:

31But they that wait upon the LORD shall renew *their* strength; they shall mount up with wings as eagles; they shall run, and not be weary; *and* they shall walk, and not faint.

Isaiah 41:10

Fear thou not; for I *am* with thee: be not dismayed; for I *am* thy God: I will strengthen thee; yea, I will help thee; yea, I will uphold thee with the right hand of my righteousness.

Isaiah 43:1-2

But now thus saith the LORD that created thee, O Jacob, and he that formed thee, O Israel, Fear not: for I have redeemed thee, I have called *thee* by thy name; thou *art* mine.

2When thou passest through the waters, I *will be* with thee; and through the rivers, they shall not overflow thee: when thou walkest through the fire, thou shalt not be burned; neither shall the flame kindle upon thee.

Jeremiah 29:11

For I know the thoughts that I think toward you, saith the LORD, thoughts of peace, and not of evil, to give you an expected end.

Lament. 3:22-26

It is of the LORD'S mercies that we are not consumed, because his compassions fail not.

23*They are* new every morning: great *is* thy faithfulness.

24The LORD *is* my portion, saith my soul; therefore will I hope in him.

25The LORD *is* good unto them that wait for him, to the soul *that* seeketh him.

26*It is* good that *a man* should both hope and quietly wait for the salvation of the LORD.

Matthew 11:28-30

Come unto me, all *ye* that labour and are heavy laden, and I will give you rest.

29Take my yoke upon you, and learn of me; for I am meek and
lowly in heart: and ye shall find rest unto your souls.

30For my yoke *is* easy, and my burden is light.

Matthew 10:30-31

But the very hairs of your head are all numbered.

31Fear ye not therefore, ye are of more value than many sparrows.

John 10:27-29

My sheep hear my voice, and I know them, and they follow me:

28And I give unto them eternal life; and they shall never perish,
neither shall any *man* pluck them out of my hand.

29My Father, which gave *them* me, is greater than all; and no *man*
is able to pluck *them* out of my Father's hand.

John 11:25-26

Jesus said unto her, I am the resurrection, and the life: he that
believeth in me, though he were dead, yet shall he live:

26And whosoever liveth and believeth in me shall never die.
Believest thou this?

John 14:27

Peace I leave with you, my peace I give unto you: not as the world giveth, give I unto you. Let not your heart be troubled, neither let it be afraid.

John 16:22

And ye now therefore have sorrow: but I will see you again, and your heart shall rejoice, and your joy no man taketh from you.

John 17:24

Father, I will that they also, whom thou hast given me, be with me where I am; that they may behold my glory, which thou hast given me: for thou lovedst me before the foundation of the world.

Romans 8:28

And we know that all things work together for good to them that love God, to them who are the called according to *his* purpose.

Romans 8:35-39

Who shall separate us from the love of Christ? *shall* tribulation, or
distress, or persecution, or famine, or nakedness, or peril, or sword?
36As it is written, For thy sake we are killed all the day long; we
are accounted as sheep for the slaughter.
37Nay, in all these things we are more than conquerors through
him that loved us.
38For I am persuaded, that neither death, nor life, nor angels, nor
principalities, nor powers, nor things present, nor things to come,
39Nor height, nor depth, nor any other creature, shall be able to
separate us from the love of God, which is in Christ Jesus our Lord.

1 Cor. 15:55-58

O death, where *is* thy sting? O grave, where *is* thy victory?
56The sting of death *is* sin; and the strength of sin *is* the law.
57But thanks *be* to God, which giveth us the victory through our
Lord Jesus Christ.
58Therefore, my beloved brethren, be ye stedfast, unmovable,
always abounding in the work of the Lord, forasmuch as ye know that
your labour is not in vain in the Lord.

2 Cor. 1:3-4

Blessed *be* God, even the Father of our Lord Jesus Christ, the Father of mercies, and the God of all comfort;

4 Who comforteth us in all our tribulation, that we may be able to comfort them which are in any trouble, by the comfort wherewith we ourselves are comforted of God.

2 Cor. 4:16-18

For which cause we faint not; but though our outward man perish, yet the inward *man* is renewed day by day.

17 For our light affliction, which is but for a moment, worketh for us a far more exceeding *and* eternal weight of glory;

18 While we look not at the things which are seen, but at the things which are not seen: for the things which are seen *are* temporal; but the things which are not seen *are* eternal.

2 Cor. 5:1-8

For we know that if our earthly house of *this* tabernacle were dissolved, we have a building of God, an house not made with hands, eternal in the heavens.

2For in this we groan, earnestly desiring to be clothed upon with our house which is from heaven:

3If so be that being clothed we shall not be found naked.

4For we that are in *this* tabernacle do groan, being burdened: not for that we would be unclothed, but clothed upon, that mortality might be swallowed up of life.

5Now he that hath wrought us for the selfsame thing *is* God, who also hath given unto us the earnest of the Spirit.

6Therefore *we are* always confident, knowing that, whilst we are at home in the body, we are absent from the Lord:

7(For we walk by faith, not by sight:)

8We are confident, *I say,* and willing rather to be absent from the body, and to be present with the Lord.

2 Cor. 12:9

And he said unto me, My grace is sufficient for thee: for my strength is made perfect in weakness. Most gladly therefore will I rather glory in my infirmities, that the power of Christ may rest upon me.

Philip. 4:6

Be careful for nothing; but in every thing by prayer and supplication with thanksgiving let your requests be made known unto God.

Philip. 4:13

I can do all things through Christ which strengtheneth me.

1 Thes. 4:13-18

But I would not have you to be ignorant, brethren, concerning them which are asleep, that ye sorrow not, even as others which have no hope.

14For if we believe that Jesus died and rose again, even so them also which sleep in Jesus will God bring with him.

15For this we say unto you by the word of the Lord, that we which are alive *and* remain unto the coming of the Lord shall not prevent them which are asleep.

16For the Lord himself shall descend from heaven with a shout, with the voice of the archangel, and with the trump of God: and the dead in Christ shall rise first:

17Then we which are alive *and* remain shall be caught up together with them in the clouds, to meet the Lord in the air: and so shall we ever be with the Lord.

18Wherefore comfort one another with these words.

Hebrews 2:9

But we see Jesus, who was made a little lower than the angels for the suffering of death, crowned with glory and honour; that he by the grace of God should taste death for every man.

Hebrews 4:15-16

For we have not an high priest which cannot be touched with the feeling of our infirmities; but was in all points tempted like as *we are, yet* without sin.

16Let us therefore come boldly unto the throne of grace, that we may obtain mercy, and find grace to help in time of need.

Hebrews 11:13

These all died in faith, not having received the promises, but having seen them afar off, and were persuaded of *them,* and embraced *them,* and confessed that they were strangers and pilgrims on the earth.

1 Peter 1:3-5

Blessed *be* the God and Father of our Lord Jesus Christ, which according to his abundant mercy hath begotten us again unto a lively hope by the resurrection of Jesus Christ from the dead,

4 To an inheritance incorruptible, and undefiled, and that fadeth not away, reserved in heaven for you,

5 Who are kept by the power of God through faith unto salvation ready to be revealed in the last time.

1 Peter 5:10-14

But the God of all grace, who hath called us unto his eternal glory by Christ Jesus, after that ye have suffered a while, make you perfect, stablish, strengthen, settle *you.*

11 To him *be* glory and dominion for ever and ever. Amen.

12 By Silvanus, a faithful brother unto you, as I suppose, I have written briefly, exhorting, and testifying that this is the true grace of God wherein ye stand.

13The *church that is* at Babylon, elected together with *you,*
saluteth you; and *so doth* Marcus my son.

14Greet ye one another with a kiss of charity. Peace *be* with you
all that are in Christ Jesus. Amen.

1 John 3:1-2

Behold, what manner of love the Father hath bestowed upon us, that we should be called the sons of God: therefore the world knoweth us not, because it knew him not.

2Beloved, now are we the sons of God, and it doth not yet appear
what we shall be: but we know that, when he shall appear, we shall be
like him; for we shall see him as he is.

Rev. 21:1-5

And I saw a new heaven and a new earth: for the first heaven and the first earth were passed away; and there was no more sea.

2And I John saw the holy city, new Jerusalem, coming down from
God out of heaven, prepared as a bride adorned for her husband.

3And I heard a great voice out of heaven saying, Behold, the
tabernacle of God *is* with men, and he will dwell with them, and they

shall be his people, and God himself shall be with them, *and be* their God.

4And God shall wipe away all tears from their eyes; and there
shall be no more death, neither sorrow, nor crying, neither shall there
be any more pain: for the former things are passed away.
5And he that sat upon the throne said, Behold, I make all things
new. And he said unto me, Write: for these words are true and
faithful.

Footprints in the Sand

Author unknown

One night a man had a dream.
He dreamed he was walking along the beach with the Lord.
Across the sky flashed scenes from his life.
For each scene, he noticed two sets of footprints in the sand:
One belonging to him, and the other to the Lord.
When the last scene of his life flashed before him,
He looked back at the footprints in the sand.
He noticed that many times along the path of his life
There was only one set of footprints.
He also noticed that it happened at the very lowest and saddest times in his life.
This really bothered him, and he questioned the Lord about it.
"Lord, you said that once I decided to follow you,
You'd walk with me all the way.
But I have noticed that during the most troublesome times in my life
There is only one set of footprints.
I don't understand why when I needed you the most you would leave me."
The Lord replied, "My precious child,
I love you and I would never leave you.
During your times of trial and suffering,
When you see only one set of footprints in the sand,
It was then that I carried you.

About the Author

Dr. Mary Ann Braham, of Clarksburg, Maryland, earned her Bachelor's Degree in Theology, a Master's Degree in Ministry, and a Doctorate in Christian Counseling from Andersonville Baptist Seminary in Camilla, Georgia. She has been involved in many areas of ministry, with a calling in ministry to the sick. Dr. Braham has accepted 2 Corinthians 1:3-4 as her life's mission.

Dr. Braham received her training in Clinical Pastoral Education at the National Institutes of Health in Bethesda, Maryland. While there she trained as chaplain in Pediatric oncology and adult neurology.

Dr. Braham is founder of Rolling Green Ministries. The focus of this ministry is to provide counseling and ministry to the sick and their families.

Lightning Source UK Ltd.
Milton Keynes UK
UKOW04f1300270215

246950UK00001B/72/P